Best of *The Daly News*

Selected Essays from the Leading Blog in Steady State Economics, 2010-2018

Edited by Brian Czech

STEADY STATE PRESS
steadystate.org

Best of *The Daly News*: Selected Essays from the Leading Blog in Steady State Economics, 2010-2018

Brian Czech (Editor)

Published by:
Steady State Press
4601 N. Fairfax Dr., Suite 1200
Arlington, VA 22203
USA

Cover Design: Elisabeth Heissler

A CIP record for this book is available from the Library of Congress Cataloging-in-Publication Data

ISBN-13: 978-1-7329933-0-3

Printed in USA

STEADY STATE PRESS
steadystate.org

Contents

Preface

Anyone familiar with CASSE—the Center for the Advancement of the Steady State Economy—will recognize the moniker and meaning of "*Daly News*." In fact, many are familiar with CASSE only *because* of *The Daly News*. They discovered the CASSE website and mission via this or that *Daly News* article, which they typically encountered by searching the web for material on limits to growth, ecological economics, sustainability in general, and, of course, the steady state economy per se.

For newcomers, "*Daly News*" was a play on words for capitalizing on the good name of Herman Daly, the champion of steady-state economics. Daly brought instant credibility to CASSE as a blog contributor and board member. Many feel that Daly—the professor emeritus at the University of Maryland, one-time senior economist at the World Bank, and winner of prestigious awards (including the Lifetime Achievement Award from the National Council for Science and the Environment)—is on the watch list for a Nobel Prize.

While CASSE had published various online materials since its establishment in 2003, the 2010 launching of *The Daly News* as CASSE's blog marked a palpable uptick in CASSE communications. From 2010–2018 (when the blog transitioned into the *Steady State Herald*) we published 304 articles, with Daly and I penning 59 apiece. Brent Blackwelder was also a regular (usually monthly) contributor as was Rob Dietz for several years. James Magnus-Johnston and Eric Zencey were frequent guest contributors.

For close to a decade, then, *The Daly News* was the flagship communications tool for CASSE. We proved there was plenty of news—not to mention opinions—on limits to growth and/or the steady state economy. Our articles ranged far and wide in style and substance. We came at our topics from philosophical, theological, ecological, economic, historical, political, sociological, and psychological angles.

We used every tenor from sober policy prescriptions to political opining to hyperbolic parody. We celebrated anniversaries and we posted obituaries. We covered the terrain from local to global. Through it all, we kept to the tenets of a non-profit educational organization as outlined in the U.S. Internal Revenue Code. We never lobbied for a candidate, but we sure critiqued a number of them all across the political spectrum.

We should all—producers and consumers of *The Daly News*—thank Herman Daly for the privilege of using his name. Those familiar with Herman's modesty won't be surprised that he was quite opposed to naming the blog after him. He had to be persuaded (and somewhat outvoted). But with Herman's name gracing our blog, each new article came out of the starting blocks with the traction of credibility.

Of course, the quality of *The Daly News* wasn't merely a matter of moniker. Quality starts with the capability of authors, and in addition to Daly, we had assembled a solid cast of writers. Brent Blackwelder, the founder of American Rivers and longtime president of Friends of the Earth, added his own brand of cachet. More importantly, though, he consistently provided a wealth of facts and insight on the environmental impacts of growth and the politics behind pro-growth policies.

Rob Dietz, an earlier co-worker of mine at the U.S. Fish and Wildlife Service, was recruited in 2007 as CASSE's executive director, and his duties included the editorial management of *The Daly News*. Dietz resigned in 2012 but was retained in a consulting capacity as the managing editor of *The Daly News* for another two years. He was a reliable and productive editor, and a creative contributor in his own right. He went on to a position with the Post-Carbon Institute, a CASSE ally closer to his preferred coordinates in Oregon.

Meanwhile, James Magnus-Johnston was winding his way through his graduate curriculum. This eventually led him to a lecturer position at Canadian Mennonite University (CMU) in 2013, as well as a board position with Assiniboine Credit Union, and appointment to the Directorship of CMU's new Centre for Resilience. His crystal-clear writing was always welcomed at *The Daly News*. After the blog ran its course, Magnus-Johnston was appointed Chief Economist of CASSE (a volunteer position) in 2018 and enrolled in the Ph.D. program at McGill University in 2019.

Eric Zencey was a wide-ranging, deep-thinking scholar and lecturer at the University of Vermont and Washington University in St. Louis. He was a prolific writer and occasionally penned a piece for *The Daly News*. Tragically, Zencey fell to cancer in 2019 after living with the disease for over ten years. He will be sorely missed, professionally and personally. He was brilliant, articulate, witty, and lovable.

My own contributions to *The Daly News* were meted out during nights and weekends while serving as a conservation biologist in the headquarters of the U.S. Fish and Wildlife Service. As a civil servant, I was prohibited from even mentioning the conflict between economic growth and environmental protection, so I had established CASSE to wear another hat when needed. Serving also as a visiting professor at Virginia Tech, I had three hats to shuffle depending on the venue. In other words, I pushed the envelope around the margins of my federal career and especially in the pages of *The Daly News*.

What do we hope to accomplish with *Best of The Daly News*? The first would be increased circulation of the articles therein. Unfortunately, circulation can't be left to clever monikers *or* capable authorship. Circulation takes strategy, effort, and financial support. Small blogs such as *The Daly News*—which operate on a shoestring budget with software to match—are difficult to cultivate among the factory-farmed, industrial-strength webpages of the World Wide Web. *The Daly News* was no stranger to malfunction, hacking, and the steep learning curve of "search engine optimization." The functionality of the commenting software was always a crapshoot. Many, if not most, articles had no extra promotion after being launched into the ether. The upshot is, *The Daly News* articles (especially the best thereof) deserve another run with a wider audience. It's not so much about CASSE deserving it but rather the audience.

Second, *Best of The Daly News* will comprise a long-awaited CASSE membership benefit. Many who have joined CASSE through the online membership process have probably wondered, "What's the difference between joining and donating?" The short answer used to be a sheepish "Not much." Now, however, membership will come with one's very own copy of the book, and it would be hard to imagine a book more apropos for this purpose.

Third, *Best of The Daly News* is the perfect production for launching the Steady State Press, CASSE's new book publishing division. The book's contents will give readers a good idea of the scope of steady-state economics and "steady statesmanship." Although a few of Herman Daly's articles occupy the deeper end of the philosophical pool, most of the book should be easy reading, so we won't scare readers away from future titles. And, frankly, we somewhat hedge our bets by including six distinctive styles of authorship. Just about anyone concerned with or interested in limits to growth, ecological economics, economic sustainability, the distribution of wealth, technological progress, national security, or international politics will find something interesting here, if not intriguing and compelling.

Two disclaimers are in order. First, the wording in *Best of The Daly News* may not match, verbatim, the online pages of *The Daly News*. Most of the articles published herein have undergone at least minor editing for purposes of updating, consistency, or segueing from one article to the next. Second, due to copyrighting issues and the exorbitant expense of printing color photos and figures, we have included none of the images found in the online articles.

Readers who enjoy the *Best of The Daly News*—as we think most will—may want to scan the rest of *The Daly News* in the online CASSE archives. (Just because the best is in this volume doesn't mean the rest is bad.) Visitors can also subscribe to the *Steady State Herald*, the CASSE blog as renamed in 2018.

With the *Best of The Daly News* under our belt and the *Steady State Herald* ushering in a new phase of steady-state journalism, CASSE will continue to play a leading role in the transition from catastrophic growth-mongering to steady statesmanship in national politics and international affairs. Will CASSE include you in some capacity? Perhaps as a member, advisor, donor, guest writer, intern, volunteer, or even an employee?

Perhaps indeed, inspired by the *Best of The Daly News*.

Acknowledgements

CASSE personnel including Casey Reiland (Managing Editor), Skyler Perkins (Projects Manager), and Benjamin Valdez (Editorial Intern) provided expert and cheerful assistance with review, editing, and production. Christine Stroud (Autumn House Press), Dana Wiser (Plough Publishing), and Sharon Donovan were helpful with book-publishing advice. Elisabeth Heissler (cover design) was a pleasure to work with. Finally, neither the book nor the Steady State Press would exist without the encouragement and support of Peter Seidel.

Brian Czech, Center for the Advancement of the Steady State Economy
Arlington, Virginia

Part I

Herman Daly

Wealth, Illth, and Net Welfare

Well-being should be counted in net terms, that is to say we should consider not only the accumulated stock of wealth but also that of "illth;" and not only the annual flow of goods but also that of "bads." The fact that we have to stretch English usage to find words like illth and bads to name the negative consequences of production that should be subtracted from the positive consequences is indicative of our having ignored the realities for which these words are the necessary names. Bads and illth consist of things like nuclear wastes, the dead zone in the Gulf of Mexico, biodiversity loss, climate change from excess greenhouse gas emissions, depleted mines, eroded topsoil, dry wells, exhausting and dangerous labor, congestion, etc. We are indebted to John Ruskin for the word "illth," and to an anonymous economist, perhaps Kenneth Boulding, for the word "bads."

In the empty world of the past, these concepts and the names for them were not needed because the economy was so small relative to the containing natural world that our production did not incur any significant opportunity cost of displaced nature. We now live in a full world, full of us and our stuff, and such costs must be counted and netted out against the benefits of growth. Otherwise we might end up with extra bads outweighing extra goods and increases in illth greater than the increases in wealth. What used to be economic growth could become uneconomic growth—that is, growth in production for which marginal costs are greater than marginal benefits, growth that in reality makes us poorer, not richer. No one is against being richer. The question is, does more growth really make us richer, or has it

3

started to make us poorer?

I suspect it is now making us poorer, at least in some high-GDP countries, and we have not recognized it. Indeed, how could we when our national accounting measures only "economic activity"? Activity is not separated into costs and benefits. Everything is added in GDP, nothing subtracted. The reason that bads and illth, inevitable joint products with goods and wealth, are not counted, even when no longer negligible in the full world, is that obviously no one wants to buy them, so there is no market for them, hence no price by which to value them. But it is worse: These bads are real and people are very willing to buy the anti-bads that protect them from the bads. For example, pollution is an unpriced, uncounted bad, but pollution cleanup is an anti-bad which is accounted as a good. Pollution cleanup has a price, and we willingly pay it up to a point and add it to GDP—but without having subtracted the negative value of the pollution itself that made the cleanup necessary. Such asymmetric accounting hides more than it reveals.

In addition to asymmetric accounting of anti-bads, we count natural capital depletion as if it were income, further misleading ourselves. If we cut down all the trees this year, catch all the fish, burn all the oil and coal, etc., then GDP counts all that as this year's income. But true income is defined (after the British economist Sir John Hicks) as the maximum that a community can consume this year and still produce and consume the same amount next year. In other words, it entails maximizing production while maintaining intact future capacity to produce. Nor is it only depletion of natural capital that is falsely counted as income; failure to maintain and replace depreciation of man-made capital, such as roads and bridges, has the same effect. Much of what we count in GDP is capital consumption and anti-bads.

As argued above, one reason that growth may be uneconomic is that we discover that its neglected costs are greater than we thought. Another reason is that we discover that the extra benefits of growth are less than we thought. This second reason has been emphasized in the studies of self-evaluated happiness, which show that beyond a threshold annual income of some $20-25,000, further growth does not increase happiness. Happiness, beyond this threshold, is overwhelmingly a function of the quality of our relationships in community by which our very identity is constituted, rather than the quantity of goods consumed. A relative increase in one's income still yields extra individual happiness, but aggregate growth is powerless to increase everyone's relative income. Growth in pursuit of relative income is like an arms race in which one party's advance cancels that of the other. It's like everyone standing and craning their neck in a football stadium while having no better view than if everyone had remained comfortably seated.

As aggregate growth beyond sufficiency loses its power to increase welfare, it increases its power to produce illth. This is because to maintain the same rate of growth, ever more matter and energy has to be mined and processed through the economy, resulting in more depletion, more waste, and requiring the use of ever more powerful and violent technologies to mine the ever leaner and less accessible deposits. Petroleum from an easily accessible well in East Texas costs less labor and capital to extract, and, therefore, directly adds less to GDP, than petroleum from an inaccessible well a mile under the Gulf of Mexico. The extra labor and capital spent to extract a barrel in the Gulf of Mexico is not a good or an addition to wealth—it is more like an anti-bad made necessary by the bad of depletion, the loss of a natural subsidy to the economy. In a full-employment economy, the extra labor and capital going to petroleum extraction would be taken from other sectors, so aggregate real GDP would likely fall. But the petroleum sector would increase its contribution to GDP as nature's subsidy to it diminished. We would be tempted to regard it as more, rather than less, productive.

The next time some economist or politician tells you we must do everything we can to grow (in order to fight poverty, win wars, colonize space, cure cancer, whatever...), remind him or her that when something grows it gets bigger! Ask him how big he thinks the economy is now, relative to the ecosphere, and how big he thinks it should be. And what makes him think that growth is still causing wealth to increase faster than illth? How does he know that we have not already entered the era of uneconomic growth? And if we have, then is not the solution to poverty to be found in sharing now, rather than in the empty promise of growth in the future?

Fitting the Name to the Named

T here may well be a better name than "steady state economy," but both the classical economists (especially John Stuart Mill) and the past few decades of discussion, not to mention CASSE's good work, have given considerable currency to "steady state economy" both as concept and name. Also, both the name and concept of a "steady state" are independently familiar to demographers, population biologists, and physicists. The classical economists used the term "stationary state" but meant by it exactly what we mean by steady state economy; briefly, a constant population and stock of physical wealth. We have added the condition that these stocks should be maintained constant by a low rate of throughput (of matter and energy), one that is well within the regenerative and assimilative capacities of the ecosystem. Any new name for this idea should be sufficiently better to compensate for losing the advantages of historical continuity and interdisciplinary familiarity. Also, "steady state economy" conveys the recognition of biophysical constraints and the intention to live within them economically, which is exactly why it can't help evoking some initial negative reaction in a growth-dominated world. There is an honesty and forthright clarity about the term "steady state economy" that should not be sacrificed to the short-term political appeal of vagueness.

A confusion arises with neoclassical growth economists' use of the term "steady-state growth" to refer to the case where labor and capital grow at the same rate, thus maintaining a constant ratio of labor to capital, even though both absolute magnitudes are growing. This should have been called "proportional growth," or perhaps "steady growth." The term "steady-state growth" is inept because growth is a process, not a state, not even a state of dynamic equilibrium.

Having made my terminological preference clear, I should add that there is nothing wrong with other people using various preferred synonyms, as long as we all mean basically the same thing. Steady state, stationary state, dynamic equilibrium, microdynamic-macrostatic economy, development without growth, degrowth, post-growth economy, economy of permanence, "new" economy, "mature" economy...these are all in use already, including by me at times. I have learned that English usage evolves quite independently of me, although like others I keep trying to "improve" it for both clarity and rhetorical advantage. If some other term catches on and becomes dominant then so be it, as long as it denotes the reality we agree on. Let a thousand synonyms bloom and linguistic natural selection will go to work. Also, it is good to remind sister organizations that their favorite term, when actually defined, is usually a close synonym to steady state economy. If it is not, then we have a difference of substance rather than of terminology.

Out of France now comes the "degrowth" (*décroissance*) movement. This arises from the recognition that the present scale of the economy is too large to be maintained in a steady state—its required throughput exceeds the regenerative and assimilative capacities of the ecosystem of which it is a part. This is almost certainly true. Nevertheless "degrowth," just like growth, is a temporary process for reaching an optimal or at least sustainable scale that we then should strive to maintain in a steady state.

Some say it is senseless to advocate a steady state unless we first have attained, or can at least specify, the optimal level at which to remain stationary. On the contrary, it is useless to know the optimum unless we first know how to live in a steady state. Otherwise knowing the optimum level will just allow us to wave goodbye to it as we grow beyond it, or as we "degrow" below it.

Optimal level is one thing; optimal growth *rate* is something else. Once we have reached the optimal level then the optimal growth rate is zero. If we are below the optimal level the temporary optimal growth rate is at least known to be positive; if we are above the optimal level we at least know that the temporary growth rate should be negative. But the first order of business is to recognize the long-run necessity of the steady state and to stop positive growth. Once we have done that, then we can worry about how to "degrow" to a more sustainable level, and how fast.

There is really no conflict between the steady state economy and "degrowth" because no one advocates negative growth as a permanent process; and no one advocates trying to maintain a steady state at the unsustainable present scale of population and consumption. But many people do advocate continuing positive growth beyond the present excessive scale, and they are the ones in control and who need to be confronted by a united opposition!

Nicholas Georgescu-Roegen, adopted by the "degrowth" movement as its posthumous founder, indeed recognized that the very long-run growth rate must be negative given the entropy law and the final dissolution of the universe. But he did not advocate speeding up that cosmic result by negative growth as an economic policy, nor for that matter did he advocate a steady state economy! In fact, he speculated that the destiny of mankind might be to have a short, fiery, and exciting life rather than a long and uneventful one. He did, however, tentatively suggest a "minimal bio-economic program" that would surely reduce growth. In general, he was interested in what is possible more than in what is desirable. The question—given the limits of the possible, what is the most desirable policy for mankind?—was not his main focus, although he did not entirely ignore it. The closest he came to explicitly dealing with that question was in the following footnote: "Is it not true that mankind's problem is to economize S (a stock) for as large an amount of life as possible, which implies to minimize s_i (a flow) for some 'good life'" (Georgescu-Roegen 1975:368)?

In other words, should we not strive to maximize cumulative lives ever to be lived over time by depleting S (terrestrial low-entropy stocks) at an annual rate that is low, but sufficient for a "good life"? There is no point in maximizing years lived in misery, so the qualification "for a good life" is important. I have always thought that Georgescu-Roegen should have put that question in bold in the text, rather than hiding it in a footnote. True enough, eventually S will be gone, and mankind will revert to what he called "a berry-picking economy" until the sun burns out, if not driven to extinction sooner by some other event. But in the meantime, striving for a steady state at a resource use rate sufficient for a good (but not luxurious) life seems to me a worthy goal, a goal of maximizing the cumulative life satisfaction possible under limited total resource constraints. This puts at the very center of economics the questions:

- How much resource use per capita is sufficient for a good life?
- How do we ensure that everyone gets that amount?
- How large a population can be supported at that standard of consumption without sacrificing carrying capacity and future life?

Needless to say, these questions have not been central to modern economics—indeed, not even peripheral!

Georgescu-Roegen did not like the idea of "sustainability" any more than that of a steady state economy because he interpreted both to mean "ecological salvation" or perpetual life for our species on earth, which of course flies in the teeth of the entropy law. And he was right about that. So, sustainability should be understood as longevity, not eternal species-life. Clear scientific thinking about "forever" seems, interestingly, to lead to the religious model of death and resurrection, and/or new creation, not perpetual continuation of this creation. Perpetuity in this world is just a glorified perpetual motion machine! To think about forever we must cross from science into theology. But longevity (a long and good life for both individual and species), even if it falls short of forever, or "ecological salvation," is still a worthy goal both for scientists and theologians, not to mention economists. A steady state economy is arguably the best strategy for achieving longevity—regardless of what we call it.

References

Georgescu-Roegen, N. 1975. Energy and economic myths. *Southern Economic Journal* 41(3):347-381.

Not Production, Not Consumption, but Transformation

W ell-established words can be misleading. In economics "production" and "consumption" are such common terms that it
is easy to forget that they do not really mean what they literally
say. Physically we do not produce anything; we just use energy to rearrange
matter into a more useful form. Production really means transformation of
what is already here. Likewise, consumption merely reflects the disarrange-
ment of carefully structured materials by the wear and tear of use into a
less useful form—another transformation, this time from useful product
into worn out product and waste.

Of course one might say that we are producing and consuming "value"
or "utility," not really physical things. However, value is always added to
something physical, namely resources, by labor and capital, which are also
physical things ultimately made from the same low-entropy energy and
materials that go into products. Nor does the service sector escape physical
dimensions—services are always rendered by something or somebody. To
abstract from physical dimensions and focus only on utility is to throw out
the baby and pour bathwater on the diaper

If we were to speak of a "transformation function" rather than a production function then we would naturally have to specify what is being
transformed, into what, by the agency of what. Natural resource flows are
transformed into flows of goods (and wastes), by the fund agents of labor
and capital. A transformation function must show both the agents of transformation (funds of labor and capital that are not themselves transformed
into the product but are needed to effect the transformation), and the flow

of resources that are indeed physically embodied in the flow of products (and waste). This distinction between fund and flow factors immediately reveals their complementary roles (i.e., as "efficient cause" and "material cause" in Aristotelian terms). Any substitution between them is very limited.

You cannot bake the same cake with half the flour, eggs, etc. by doubling the number of cooks and the size of the oven. One natural resource can often substitute for another, and capital can often substitute for labor or vice versa, but more labor and capital can hardly substitute for a smaller resource flow, beyond the very limited extent of sweeping up and re-using waste such as scraps, sawdust, etc. (which ought to have already been accounted for in specifying a technically efficient production function). In most textbooks the production function depicts output as a function of inputs, undifferentiated as to their fund or flow nature, and all considered fundamentally substitutable.

But if the usual production function does not distinguish fund agents of transformation from the flow of natural resources being transformed, then how does it envisage the process of converting factor inputs into product outputs? Usually by multiplying them together, as in the Cobb-Douglas and other multiplicative functions. What could be more natural linguistically than multiplying "factors" to get a "product"? But this is mathematics, not economics. There is absolutely nothing analogous to multiplication going on in what we customarily call production—there is only transformation.

Try to multiply the resource flow by labor or capital to get product out-flow and your "production function" will have immediately run afoul of the law of conservation of mass. Perhaps to escape such incongruities most production functions contain only labor and capital, omitting resources entirely. We can now bake our cake with only cook and oven; no ingredients to be transformed at all!

How did this nonsense come into economics? I suspect it represents a confusion between the production function as a theoretical analytical description of the physical process of transformation (a recipe), and a production function as a mere statistical correlation between outputs and inputs. The latter is common in macroeconomics, the former in microeconomics, although that is not a hard and fast rule. The distinction between a theoretical description and a statistical correlation is often ignored in both contexts.

The statistical approach usually includes only labor and capital as factor inputs, and then discovers that these two factors "explain" only 60% of the historical change in output, leaving a 40% residual to be explained by "something else." No problem, say the growth economists: That large residual is "obviously" a measure of technological progress. However, the statistical residual is in fact a measure of everything that is not capital and labor—including specifically the quantity and quality of resources transformed. Increased resource use gets counted in the residual and attributed to technological progress. Then that same measure of technological progress is appealed to in order to demonstrate the unimportance of resources! If we thought in terms of a transformation function, rather than production *ex nihilo,* it would be hard to make such an error.

The basic points just made were developed more rigorously forty years ago by Nicholas Georgescu-Roegen in his fund-flow critique of the neoclassical production function. Neoclassical growth economists have never answered his critique. Why bring it up again, and what is the relevance to steady-state economics?

It is worth raising the issue again precisely because it has never been answered. What kind of a science is it that can get away with ignoring a fundamental critique for forty years? It is relevant to steady-state economics because it views production as physical transformation subject to biophysical limits and the laws of thermodynamics. Also it shows that the force of resource scarcity is in the nature of a limiting factor, and not so easy to escape by substitution of capital for resources, as often claimed by neoclassical growth economists.

The Populations Problem

The population problem should be considered from the point of view of all populations—populations of both humans and their artifacts (cars, houses, livestock, cell phones, etc.)—in short, populations of all "dissipative structures" engendered, bred, or built by humans. In other words, the populations of human bodies and of their extensions. Or in yet other words, the populations of all organs that support human life and the enjoyment thereof, both endosomatic (within the skin) and exosomatic (outside the skin) organs.

All of these organs are capital equipment that support our lives. The endosomatic equipment—heart, lungs, kidneys—support our lives quite directly. The exosomatic organs—farms, factories, electric grids, transportation networks—support our lives indirectly. One should also add "natural capital," which is exosomatic capital comprised of structures complementary to endosomatic organs, but not made by humans (e.g., forests, rivers, soil, atmosphere).

The reason for pluralizing the "population problem" to the populations of all dissipative structures is two-fold. First, all these populations require a metabolic throughput from low-entropy resources extracted from the environment and eventually returned to the environment as high-entropy wastes, encountering both depletion and pollution limits. In a physical sense the final product of the economic activity of converting nature into ourselves and our stuff, and then using up or wearing out what we have made, is waste. Second, what keeps this from being an idiotic activity, grinding up the world into waste, is the fact that all these populations of dissipative

13

structures have the common purpose of supporting the maintenance and enjoyment of life.

As A.J. Lotka pointed out, ownership of endosomatic organs is equally distributed, while the exosomatic organs are not. Ownership of the latter may be collective or individual, equally or unequally distributed. Control of these external organs may be democratic or dictatorial. Owning one's own kidneys is not enough to support one's life if one does not have access to water from rivers, lakes, or rain, either because of scarcity or monopoly ownership of the complementary exosomatic organ. Likewise, our lungs are of little value without the complementary natural capital of green plants and atmospheric stocks of oxygen. Therefore, all life-supporting organs, including natural capital, form a unity. They have a common function, regardless of whether they are located within the boundary of human skin or outside that boundary. In addition to being united by common purpose, they are also united by their role as dissipative structures. They are all physical structures whose default tendency is to dissipate or fall apart, in accordance with the entropy law.

Our standard of living is roughly measured by the ratio of outside-skin to inside-skin capital; that is, the ratio of human-made artifacts to human bodies, the ratio of one kind of dissipative structure to another kind. Within-skin capital is made and maintained overwhelmingly from renewable resources, while outside-skin capital relies heavily on nonrenewable resources. The rate of evolutionary change of endosomatic organs is exceedingly slow; the rate of change of exosomatic organs has become very rapid. In fact, the evolution of human beings is now overwhelmingly centered on exosomatic organs. This evolution is goal-directed, not random, and its driving purpose has become "economic growth," and that growth has been achieved largely by the depletion of nonrenewable resources.

Although human evolution is now decidedly purpose-driven we continue to be enthralled by neo-Darwinist aversion to teleology and devotion to random. Economic growth, by promising "more for everyone eventually," becomes the *de facto* purpose, the social glue that keeps things from falling apart. What happens when growth becomes uneconomic, increasing costs faster than benefits? How do we know that this is not already the case? If one asks such questions one is told to talk about something else, like space colonies on Mars, or unlimited energy from cold fusion, or geo-engineering, or the wonders of globalization, and to remember that all these glorious purposes require growth now in order to provide still more growth in the future. Growth is good, end of discussion, now shut up!

Let us reconsider in the light of these facts, the idea of demographic transition. By definition this is the transition from a human population maintained by high birth rates equal to high death rates to one maintained by low birth rates equal to low death rates, and, consequently, from a population with low life expectancy to one with high life expectancy. Statistically such transitions have been observed as standard of living (ratio of exosomatic to endosomatic capital) increases. Many studies have attempted to explain this fact, and much hope has been invested in it as an automatic cure for overpopulation. "Development is the best contraceptive" is a related slogan, partly based in fact, and partly in wishful thinking.

There are a couple of thoughts I'd like to add to the discussion of demographic transition. The first and most obvious one is that populations of artifacts can undergo an analogous transition from high rates of production and depreciation to low ones. The lower rates will maintain a constant population of longer-lived, more durable artifacts.

Our economy has a growth-oriented focus on maximizing production flows (birth rates of artifacts) that keeps us in the pre-transition mode, giving rise to growing artifact populations, low product lifetimes, high GDP, and high throughput, with consequent environmental destruction. The transition from a high-maintenance throughput to a low one applies to both human and artifact populations independently. From an environmental perspective, lower throughput is desirable in both cases, at least down to some distant lower limits.

The second thought I would like to add to the discussion of demographic transition is a question: Does the human transition, when induced by rising standard of living, as usually assumed, increase or decrease the total load of all dissipative structures on the environment? Specifically, if Indian fertility is to fall to the Swedish level, must Indian per capita possession of artifacts (standard of living) rise to the Swedish level? If so, would this not likely increase the total load of all dissipative structures on the Indian environment, perhaps beyond capacity to sustain the required throughput?

The point of this speculation is to suggest that "solving" the population problem by relying on the demographic transition to lower birth rates could impose a larger burden on the environment rather than the smaller burden that would be the case with direct reduction in fertility. Of course, reduction in fertility by automatic correlation with rising standard of living is politically easy, while direct fertility reduction is politically difficult. But what is politically easy may be environmentally destructive.

To put it another way, consider the "IPAT formula", or I = PAT. P, population of human bodies, is one set of dissipative structures. A, affluence, or GDP per capita, reflects another set of dissipative structures—cars, buildings, ships, toasters, iPads, etc. (not to mention populations of livestock and agricultural plants). In a finite world, some populations grow at the expense of others. Cars and humans are now competing for land, water, and sunlight to grow either food or fuel. More nonhuman dissipative structures will at some point *force* a reduction in other dissipative structures, namely human bodies. This forced demographic transition is less optimistic than the voluntary one induced by chasing a higher standard of living more effectively with fewer dependents. In an empty world, we saw the trade-off between artifacts and people as induced by desire for a higher standard of living. In the full world, that trade-off seems forced by competition for limited resources.

The usual counter to such thoughts is that we can improve the efficiency by which throughput maintains dissipative structures. We accomplish this by developing new technology—T in the IPAT formula—measured as throughput per unit of GDP. For example, a car that lasts longer and gets better mileage is still a dissipative structure, but with a more efficient metabolism that allows it to live on a lower rate of throughput.

Likewise, human organisms might be genetically redesigned to require less food, air, and water. Indeed, smaller people would be the simplest way of increasing metabolic efficiency (measured as number of people maintained by a given resource throughput). To my knowledge no one has yet suggested breeding smaller people as a way to avoid limiting births, but that probably just reflects my ignorance. We have, however, been busy breeding and genetically engineering larger and faster-growing plants and livestock. So far, the latter dissipative structures have been mostly complementary with populations of human bodies, but in a finite and full world, the relationship will soon become competitive.

Indeed, if we think of population as the cumulative number of people ever to live over time, then many artifact populations are already competitive with the human population. That is, more consumption today of terrestrial low entropy in non-vital uses (Cadillacs, rockets, weapons) means less terrestrial low entropy available for capturing solar energy tomorrow (plows, solar collectors, ecosystem regeneration). The solar energy that will still fall on the earth for millions of years after the material structures needed to capture it are dissipated will be wasted, just like the solar energy that shines on the moon.

There is a limit to how many dissipative structures the ecosphere can sustain—more endosomatic capital must ultimately displace some exosomatic capital and vice versa. Some of our exosomatic capital is critical, such as that part which can photosynthesize (i.e., the green plants). Our endosomatic capital cannot long endure without the critical exosomatic capital of green plants (along with soil and water, and of course sunlight). In sum, demographers' interest should extend to the populations of all dissipative structures, their metabolic throughputs, and the relations of complementarity and substitutability among them. Economists should analyze the supply, demand, production, and consumption of all these populations within an ecosphere that is finite, non-growing, entropic, and open only to a fixed flow of solar energy. This reflects a paradigm shift from the empty-world vision to the full-world vision—a world full of human-made dissipative structures that both depend upon and displace natural structures. Growth looks very different depending on which paradigm it is viewed from.

Carrying capacity of the ecosystem depends on how many dissipative structures of all kinds have to be carried. Some will say to others, "You can't have a glass of wine and piece of meat for dinner because I need the grain required by your fine diet to feed my three hungry children." The answer will be, "You can't have three children at the expense of my and my one child's already modest standard of living." Both have a good point. That conflict will be difficult to resolve, but we are not yet there.

Rather, now some are saying, "You can't have three houses and fly all over the world twice a year because I need the resources to feed my eight children." And the current reply is, "You can't have eight children at the expense of my small family's luxurious standard of living." In the second case neither side elicits much sympathy, and there is great room for compromise to limit both excessive population and per capita consumption. Better to face limits to both human and artifact populations before the terms of the trade-off get too harsh.

Cold War Leftovers

T hose of us old enough to remember the Cold War will also remember that it involved a growth race between Capitalism and Communism. Whichever system could grow faster would presumably win the allegiance of the uncommitted world. The idea of a steady state was therefore anathema to both sides. The communist growth god failed first because of political repression and economic inefficiency. But the capitalist growth god is now failing as growth becomes uneconomic due to environmental and social costs and is propped up only by fraudulent accounting, monopoly, and financial corruption. Neither system can accept the idea of a steady state economy, but neither can attain the impossible alternative of growing forever.

Advocates of the steady state economy are long accustomed to attacks from capitalists, which have by no means disappeared. We are less accustomed to attacks from the left, not from communists who have virtually disappeared, but from remaining Marxists and socialists. Although Marxism is largely discredited (along with other manifestations of 19th century determinism, such as Freudianism and Eugenic Darwinism), one cannot by any means take that as a vindication of capitalism, which has only gotten worse in its quest for unending growth. In spite of my overall negative view of Marxism, there are some "green Marxists" who, in my opinion, are worth reading (e.g., John Bellamy Foster, Brett Clark, and Richard York, who collaborated to author *The Ecological Rift*). Recently, another socialist (I am not sure if he considers himself a Marxist) has criticized the steady state economy for being essentially capitalist. This is economic historian

Richard Smith. He sees the steady state economy as a distraction from "eco-socialism."

One should be grateful to one's critics—it is much better to be criticized than ignored. Richard Smith kindly takes me as his exhibit A for a position that he misleadingly labels "steady-state capitalism." I have never used that term, always speaking of a steady state economy, which is neither capitalism nor socialism, although it draws features from both. Indeed, in the Cold War context it was thought to offer a Third Way, a possibility for uniting the best features of each system. Change is impossible unless you start from where you are. As noted, I am more accustomed to attacks from capitalists, so it is at least a refreshing change to be attacked, rather politely, by a socialist who, unlike many neoclassical growthists, has taken the trouble to learn about the steady state economy. Disagreements will follow, but my appreciation for his critical attention needs to be expressed.

Richard Smith characterizes capitalism as a system that must "grow or die" (Smith 2010:31). It then follows immediately that since capitalism must grow, it cannot be a steady state. OK then, if capitalism cannot be a steady state, then neither can a steady state be capitalism. So, let's not speak of "steady-state capitalism." I, for one, never have—although Mr. Smith tendentiously attributes that term to me. By the same logic, following Marx, one might define socialism as a classless society based on overwhelming material abundance arrived at through rapid economic growth under the centrally planned dictatorship of the proletariat. Socialism also depends on growth. Therefore, steady-state socialism is impossible. It was precisely to avoid such sterile definitional disputes that I always said "steady state economy," and never "steady-state capitalism," or socialism for that matter.

Would it not be more productive to start by defining a steady state economy, followed by arguments for its necessity and desirability? We could then avoid ideological classifications based on abstract definitions of what capitalism or socialism "essentially must always be." We now live in a full world. Capitalism and socialism are both from the empty-world era in which growth was the *desideratum*. Must we insist on pouring new wine into old wineskins and then watching them burst?

Smith's unhappiness with me derives most specifically from my preference for the market over centralized planning as a tool for dealing with the single technical problem of allocative efficiency. Steady-state economics deals with three problems: sustainable scale, just distribution, and efficient allocation. It takes the first two issues, scale and distribution, away from the market. It calls for quantitative ecological limits on the throughput of resources so that the market can no longer determine the physical scale of the economy relative to the biosphere. It also advocates social limits to the range of income inequality, so that the market can no longer generate large inequalities of wealth. Subject to these two prior macro-level aggregate constraints, it then relies on the market to efficiently allocate resources. This is not advocacy of the Market with a capital *M*, the deified master evaluator and controller of life. This is market with a small *m*, a limited tool for rationing, communicating, and exchanging goods and services.

Reliance on markets for allocation (now within prior ecological and distributional limits) is further constrained, even within traditional microeconomics, by opposition to monopoly and restriction of market allocation to rival and excludable goods. Non-rival and public goods have long been recognized to require some degree of non-market allocation. Even so, Mr. Smith seems unhappy with *any* role for markets.

Richard Smith deserves credit for recognizing and opposing the real evils of financial, monopolizing, crony capitalism as it currently exists. And, unlike both traditional Marxists and neoclassical economists, he realizes that we cannot grow forever, and that we have in many dimensions already far overshot optimal scale. And he takes the trouble to debate critical issues rather than ignore them. However, he thinks only socialism can somehow cure these evils. The operative word here is "somehow." Somehow, we must wipe the slate clean of any institutions associated with markets, such as property, division of labor, exchange, and profit. How? By violent revolution? By rational persuasion? By moral conversion? That is left vague. It is all very well, for example, to point out the real problems with excess reliance on the profit motive. But if we abolish profit as a source of income then we also abolish self-employment. Everyone must then become an employee earning a wage. Who then is the employer? Do we all then work for Ajax United Amalgamated Corporations? Or for the Universal State Monopoly? Is there something about the mere act of exchange and the category of profit (not just excessive inequality and monopoly ownership of the means of production) that offends or confuses Marxists?

Nevertheless, if Marxists now advocate limiting growth, that is a big change. Maximizing growth to achieve overwhelming material abundance has been seen as the path to the "new socialist man," who, according to Marx, can only be freed from his bourgeois greed by objective abundance, by the abolition of scarcity, not by the "utopian" morality of sharing. I have never seen a Marxist proposal to limit the scale of the macroeconomy to an ecologically sustainable level—nor for a maximum as well as a minimum income to limit the range of distributive inequality to a reasonable and fair degree. Rhetorical calls for absolute equality and abolition of private property abound, but are neither realistic nor fair.

Marxists also go far out of their way not to recognize overpopulation and the need to limit population growth (a critical dimension of both scale and distributive inequality, given class differentials in fertility and access to contraception). A stationary population is part of the definition of a steady state economy. Furthermore, a limited range of income inequality would restrict the ability of the rich to bid necessities away from the poor in the market. Unjust distribution of income does get reflected in markets, but let us attack the cause, not the symptom. And quotas on basic resource throughput could raise prices enough to eliminate most frivolous and wasteful production, as well as stimulate recycling, and increase efficiency while ruling out the Jevons effect. If we start with depletion quotas on basic resources, then the resulting increase in resource prices and efficiency cannot lead to more use of the resource. Auctioning transferrable quotas rather than giving them away (markets rather than direct government allocation, *pace* Mr. Smith) will raise enough revenue to greatly reduce taxes on the poor.

It is not at all clear why Smith thinks markets must always be bad masters rather than good servants. If we forgo markets, should we then perhaps have another go at central planning and collectivization of agriculture? Would Mr. Smith have preferred War Communism to Lenin's New Economic Policy because the latter was really just "state capitalism" that re-established significant reliance on markets? To be fair, we do not know what Smith thinks about any historical experience with the abolition of markets because he does not mention any.

If "eco-socialists" reject the steady state economy as "inherently capitalistic," then what specific policies do they recommend? How do their policies differ from those of steady-state economics? Are there some policies we agree on?

Critics of the present growth economy, whether steady state economy or "eco-socialist," are, however, united in humility before a common dilemma—namely that the bought-and-paid-for government that would have to enact the programs needed for a steady state economy is the same government that would have to run a socialist economy. A government that cannot even break up too-big-to-fail monopolies, or provide debt-free money as a public utility, or even institute a carbon tax, will certainly not be able to administer a centrally planned economy—nor even a steady state. We have deeper problems of moral and spiritual renewal (in addition to recognition of finitude and laws of thermodynamics) that transcend both capitalism and socialism. It is admittedly hard to envision the source for the basic moral renewal required to face the enormous problems that are looming, but Marxist dialectical materialism and collectivism seem to already have historically demonstrated their failure in this regard. We need something new. Although things look bleak, we never know enough to justify giving up hope. But we should avoid repeating past mistakes.

References

Smith, R. 2010. Beyond growth or beyond capitalism? *Real World Economics Review* 53:28-42.

War and Peace and the Steady State Economy

My parents were children during World War I, the so-called "war to end all wars." I was a child during WWII, an adolescent during the Korean War, and except for a physical disability would likely have been drafted to fight in the Vietnam War. Then came Afghanistan, Iraq, the continuous Arab-Israeli conflict, ISIS, Ukraine, Syria, etc. Now as a senior citizen, I see that war has metastasized into terrorism. It is hard to conceive of a country at war, or threatened by terrorism, moving to a steady state economy.

Peace is necessary for real progress, including progress toward a steady state economy. While peace should be our priority, might it nevertheless be the case that working toward a steady state economy would further the goal of peace? Might growth be a major cause of war, and the steady state a necessity for eliminating that cause? I think this is so.

More people require more space (*lebensraum*) and more resources. More things per person also require more space and more resources. Recently I learned that the word "rival" derives from the same root as "river." People who get their water from the same river are rivals, at least when there are too many of them, each drawing too much.

For a while, the resource demands of growth can be met from within national borders. Then there is pressure to exploit or appropriate the global commons. Then comes the peaceful penetration of other nations' ecological space by trade. The uneven geographic distribution of resources (petroleum, fertile soil, water) causes specialization among nations and interdependence along with trade. Are interdependent nations more or less likely to go to war? That has been argued both ways, but when one growing nation has what another thinks it absolutely needs for its growth, conflict easily displaces trade. As interdependence becomes more acute, then trade becomes less voluntary and more like an offer you can't refuse. Unless trade is voluntary, it is not likely to be mutually beneficial. Top-down global economic integration replaces trade among interdependent national economies. We have been told on highest authority that because the American way of life requires foreign oil, we will have it one way or another.

International "free trade pacts" (NAFTA, TPP, TAFTA) are supposed to increase global GDP, thereby making us all richer and effectively expanding the size of the earth and easing conflict. These secretly negotiated agreements among the elites are designed to benefit private global corporations, often at the expense of the public good of nations. Some think that strengthening global corporations by erasing national boundaries will reduce the likelihood of war. More likely we will just shift to feudal corporate wars in a post-national global commons, with corporate fiefdoms effectively buying national governments and their armies, supplemented by already existing private mercenaries.

It is hard to imagine a steady state economy without peace; it is hard to imagine peace in a full world without a steady state economy. Those who work for peace are promoting the steady state, and those who work for a steady state are promoting peace. This implicit alliance needs to be made explicit. Contrary to popular belief, growth in a finite and full world is not the path to peace, but to further conflict. It is an illusion to think that we can buy peace with growth. The growth economy and warfare are now natural allies. It is time for peacemakers and steady staters to recognize their natural alliance.

It would be naïve, however, to think that growth in the face of environmental limits is the only cause of war. Evil ideologies, religious conflict, and "clash of civilizations" also cause wars. National defense is necessary, but uneconomic growth does not make our country stronger. The secular West has a hard time understanding that religious conviction can motivate people to kill and die for their beliefs. Modern devotion to the Secular God of Growth, who promises heaven on earth, has itself become a fanatical religion that inspires violence as much as any ancient Moloch. The Second Commandment, forbidding the worship of false gods (idolatry) is not outdated. Our modern idols are new versions of Mammon and Mars.

Growth, Debt, and the World Bank

W hen I was in graduate school in economics in the early 1960s, we were taught that capital was the limiting factor in growth and development. Just inject capital into the economy and it would grow. As the economy grew, you could then re-invest the growth increment as new capital and make it grow exponentially. Eventually the economy would be rich. Originally, to get things started, capital came from savings, confiscation, or foreign aid or investment, but later it would come out of the national growth increment itself. Capital embodied technology, the source of its power. Capital was magic stuff, but scarce. It all seemed convincing at the time.

Many years later when I worked for the World Bank, it was evident that capital was no longer the limiting factor, if indeed it ever had been. Trillions of dollars of capital were circling the globe looking for projects in which to become invested so the investment could grow. The World Bank understood that the limiting factor was what they called "bankable projects," concrete investments that could embody abstract financial capital and make its value grow at an acceptable rate, usually ten percent per annum or more, doubling every seven years. Since there were not enough bankable projects to absorb the available financial capital, the World Bank decided to stimulate the creation of such projects with "country development teams" set up in the borrowing countries but with World Bank technical assistance. No doubt many such projects were useful, but it was still hard to grow at ten-percent rate without involuntarily displacing people or running down natural capital and counting it as income, both of which were done on a grand scale. And the loans had to be repaid. Of course, they did get repaid, frequently not out of the earnings of the projects which were often disappointing but out of the general tax revenues of the borrowing governments. Lending to sovereign governments with the ability to tax greatly increases the likelihood of being repaid—and perhaps encourages a bit of laxity in approving projects.

Where did all this excess financial capital come from? Not from savings (China excepted) but from new money and easy credit generated by our fractional reserve banking system, amplified by increased leverage in the purchase of stocks. Recipients of new money bid resources away from existing uses by offering a higher price. If there are unemployed resources, and if the new uses are profitable, then the temporary rise in prices is offset by new production—by growth. But resource and environmental scarcity, along with a shortage of bankable projects, put the brakes on this growth and resulted in too much financial capital trying to become incarnate in too few bankable projects.

So, the World Bank had to figure out why its projects yielded low returns. The answer sketched above was ideologically unacceptable because it hinted at ecological limits to growth. A more acceptable answer soon became clear to the Bank's economists: micro-level projects could not be productive in a macro environment of irrational and inefficient government policy. The solution was to restructure the macro economies by "structural adjustment"—free trade, export-led growth, balanced budgets, strict control of inflation, elimination of social subsidies, deregulation, suspension of labor and environmental protection laws—the so-called Washington Consensus.

How to convince borrowing countries to make these painful "structural adjustments" at the macro level, to create the environment in which Bank-financed projects would be productive? The answer was, conveniently, a new form of lending, structural adjustment loans, to encourage or bribe the policy reforms stipulated by the term "structural adjustment." An added reason for structural adjustment, or "policy lending," was to move lots of dollars quickly to countries like Mexico to ease their balance of payments difficulty in repaying loans they had received from private US banks. Also, policy loans, now about half of World Bank lending, require no lengthy and expensive project planning and supervision the way project loans do. The money moves quickly. The World Bank definition of efficiency became, it seemed, "moving the maximum amount of money with the minimum amount of thought."

Why, one might ask, would a country borrow money at interest to make policy changes that it could make on its own without any loans, if it thought the policies were good ones? Maybe they did not really favor the policies, and, therefore, needed a bribe to do what was in their own best interests. Maybe the goal of the current borrowing government was simply to get the new loan, splash the money around among friends and relatives, and leave the next government to pay it back with interest.

Such thoughts got little attention at the World Bank, which was haunted by the specter of an impending "negative payments flow," that is, repayments of old loans plus interest greater than the volume of new loans. Would the World Bank eventually shrink and disappear as unnecessary? A horrible thought for any bureaucracy! But the alternative to a negative payments flow for the World Bank is ever-increasing debt for the borrowing countries. Of course the World Bank did not claim to be in the business of increasing the debt of poor countries. Rather it was fostering growth by injecting capital and increasing the debtor countries' capacity to absorb capital from outside. So what if the debt grew, as long as GDP was growing? The assumption was that the real sector could grow as fast as the financial sector, that physical wealth could grow as fast as monetary debt.

The main goal of the World Bank is to make loans, push the money out the door, and be a money pump. If financial capital were really the limiting factor, countries would line up with good projects and the World Bank would ration capital among countries. But financial capital is superabundant and good projects are scarce, so the World Bank had to actively push the money. To speed up the pump, they send country development teams out to invent projects; if the projects fail, then they invent structural adjustment loans to induce a more favorable macro environment; if structural adjustment loans are treated as bribes by corrupt borrowing governments, the World Bank does not complain too much for fear of slowing the money pump and incurring a "negative payments flow."

If capital is no longer the magic limiting factor whose presence unleashes economic growth, then what is it?

"Capital," said Frederick Soddy, "merely means unearned income divided by the rate of interest and multiplied by 100" (Soddy 2012: 27). He further explained that, "Although it may comfort the lender to think that his wealth still exists somewhere in the form of "capital," it has been or is being used up by the borrower either in consumption or investment, and no more than food or fuel can it be used again later. Rather it has become debt, an indent on future revenues..."

In other words, capital in the financial sense is the future expected net revenue from a project divided by the rate of interest and multiplied by 100. Rather than magic stuff, it is an indent, a lien, on the future real production of the economy. It is a debt to be repaid or, alternatively (and perhaps preferably), to not be repaid but kept as the source of interest payments far into the future.

Of course, debt is incurred in exchange for real resources to be used now, which as Soddy says cannot be used again in the future. But if the financed project can extract more resources employing more labor in the future to increase the total revenue of society, then the debt can be paid off with interest, with some of the extra revenue left over as profit. But this requires an increased throughput of matter and energy, and increased labor. In other words, it requires physical growth of the economy. Such growth in yesterday's empty-world economy was reasonable. In today's full-world economy it is not. It is now generally recognized that there is too much debt worldwide, both public and private. The reason so much debt was incurred is that we have had absurdly unrealistic expectations about growth. We never expected that growth itself would begin to cost us more than it was worth, making us poorer, not richer. But it did. And the only solution our economists, bankers, and politicians have come up with is more of the same! Could we not at least take a short time-out to discuss the idea of a steady state economy?

References

Soddy, F. 2012. *Cartesian Economics: The Bearing of Physical Science upon State Stewardship.* Cosimo Incorporation, New York.

Thoughts on Pope Francis's *Laudato si'*

As a Protestant Christian, my devotion to the Catholic Church has been rather minimal, based largely on respect for early church history, and for love of an aunt who was a nun. In recent times the Catholic Church's opposition to birth control, plus the pedophile and cover-up scandals, further alienated me. Like many others I first viewed Pope Francis as perhaps a breath of fresh air, but little more. After reading his encyclical on environment and justice, dare I hope that what I considered merely "fresh air" could actually be the wind of Pentecost filling the Church anew with the Spirit? Maybe. At a minimum he has given us a more truthful, informed, and courageous analysis of the environmental and moral crisis than have our secular political leaders.

True, the important question of population was conspicuous by its near absence. In an earlier offhand remark, however, Francis said that Catholics don't need to breed "like rabbits," and pointed to the Church's doctrine of responsible parenthood. Perhaps he will follow up on that in a future encyclical. In any case, most lay Catholics have for some time stopped listening to popes on contraception. The popular attitude is expressed in a cartoon showing an Italian mamma wagging her finger at the Pontiff and saying, "You no playa da game; you no maka da rules." Discussing population would not have changed realities and would have aroused official opposition and distracted attention from the major points of the encyclical. So, I will follow Francis's politic example and put the population question aside, but with a reference to historian John T. Noonan, Jr.'s classic book, *Contraception*, which sorts out the history of doctrine on this issue.

The big ideas of the encyclical are Creation care and justice and the failure of our technocratic growth economy to provide either justice or care for Creation. Also discussed was the integration of science and religion as necessary, though different, avenues to truth. And yes, the Pope supports the scientific consensus on the reality of climate change, but, media monomania to the contrary, the encyclical is about far more than that.

Francis's voice is of course not the first to come from Christians in defense of Creation. In addition to his ancient namesake from Assisi, Francis also recognized Ecumenical Patriarch Bartholomew of the Eastern Orthodox Church, who has for two decades been organizing conferences and speaking out in defense of rivers and oceans, including the Black Sea. The Orthodox Church lost a generation of believers to communistic atheism but is gaining back many young people attracted to the theology of Creation and the actions it inspires. Liberal mainline Protestant Christians, and more recently conservative Evangelicals, have also found their ecological conscience. So Francis's encyclical would seem to be a capstone that unifies the main divisions of Christianity on at least the fundamental recognition that we have a shamefully neglected duty to care for the Earth out of which we evolved and to share the Earth's life support more equitably with each other, the future, and other creatures. Many atheists also agree, while claiming that their agreement owes nothing to Judeo-Christian tradition. That is historically questionable, but their support is welcome nonetheless.

This theology of Creation should not be confused with the evolution-denying, anti-science views of some Christian biblical literalists (confusingly called "Creationists" rather than "literalists"). Mankind's duty to care for Creation, through which humans have evolved to reflect at least the faint image of their Creator, conflicts headlong with the current dominant idolatry of growthism and technological Gnosticism. The idea of duty to care for Creation also conflicts with the materialist determinism of neo-Darwinist fundamentalists who see "Creation" as the random result of multiplying infinitesimal probabilities by an infinite number of trials. The policy implication of determinism (even if stochastic) is that purposeful policy is illusory, both practically and morally.

Creation care is also incompatible with the big lie that sharing the Earth's limited resources is unnecessary because economic growth will make us all rich. Francis calls this magical thinking. He skates fairly close to the idea of steady-state economics, of qualitative development without quantitative growth in scale, although this concept is not specifically considered. Consider his paragraph 193:

In any event, if in some cases sustainable development were to involve new forms of growth, then in other cases, given the insatiable and irresponsible growth produced over many decades, we need also to think of containing growth by setting some reasonable limits and even retracing our steps before it is too late. We know how unsustainable is the behaviour of those who constantly consume and destroy, while others are not yet able to live in a way worthy of their human dignity. That is why the time has come to accept decreased growth in some parts of the world, in order to provide resources for other places to experience healthy growth.

In the last sentence "decreased growth" seems an inexact English translation from the Spanish version *"decrecimiento,"* or the Italian version *"decrescita"* (likely the original languages of the document), which should be translated as "degrowth" or negative growth, which is of course stronger than "decreased growth."

Laudato si' is already receiving both strong support and resistance. The resistance testifies to the radical nature of Francis's renewal of the basic doctrine of the Earth and cosmos as God's Creation. Pope Francis will be known by the enemies this encyclical makes for him, and these enemies may well be his strength. So far in the USA they are not an impressive lot: the Heartland Institute, Jeb Bush, Senator James Inhofe, Rush Limbaugh, Rick Santorum, and others. Unfortunately, they represent billions in special-interest money and have a big corporate-media megaphone. The encyclical calls out the opponents and forces them to defend themselves. To give them the benefit of the doubt, they may really think that Francis is rendering to God what actually belongs to Caesar's oligarchy. But neither Caesar, nor the market, nor technology created us and the earth that sustains us. Thanks to Francis for making that very clear when so many are denying it, either explicitly or implicitly.

Part II

Brian Czech

Limits to Growth—of Stuff, Value, and GDP

I 'm starting to think that perpetual growth notions are the Achilles heel of the human brain. They pop up like munchkins on a Whack-a-Mole machine. You smash one, and up come two.

A recent example comes from Tim Worstall, a business and technology writer for *Forbes*. Like the long lineage of *Homo polyannas* before him, he assures his poor readers that we can have perpetually growing GDP without using more resources. He uses a variety of the old "growth is more value, not stuff" argument.

Worstall says, "It really is true that as value increases we have economic growth. And how are we determining that value? Through the market prices that people are willing to pay for them. And what is the determinant of that? Well, actually, it's us. Our own often arbitrary and always subjective estimations of what something is worth to us. Which isn't, as I hope can be seen, something that is bounded by any physical limit at all" (Worstall 2012).

Now I don't know about you, but when someone is compelled to announce, "It really is true," my "Prove It" flag pops up. And sure enough, Mr. Worstall has a lot to prove.

For starters, just exactly what evidence does Mr. Worstall have to support his notion that our estimations of value are unbounded? I don't recall having or hearing of an experience where something seemed to increase in value more, more yet, and forevermore. Do you? Now it may have seemed that way for some short period of time with something like coffee. But unless you're moving into ecstasy ad nauseam—an oxymoron if there ever was one—the value of the experience was bounded, right?

Why can't Worstall and the perpetual growthers just face it with the rest of us: life is all about limits. Life, death, taxes, and limits. What's wrong with limits, anyway? If there weren't any, what value would a certain level of progress or satisfaction have? How would you measure it?

Now sure, you might "value" living more as you get closer to dying. You might try to measure this value and say, "I'm twice as concerned with living now." You might even spend twice as much money on health food. That's fine and understandable, but it's not economic growth. If you spent more on health food, you had less to spend on coffee, chiropractic, or bingo at the Elks Club.

That brings us to an even bigger burden of proof begged by Mr. Worstall. The main point of his article is that all this ever-increasing appreciation or satisfaction or happiness, which requires not one jot or tittle of energy or material, will result in GDP growth! This, he lectures the scientists, is really what GDP growth is all about: increasing value where value may increase without increasing use of energy and material.

Where's the proof? Have we ever seen GDP increase without increasing use of energy and material? If the Worstalls of the world would only put their money where their mouths were, we could cap energy and material flows and test their hypothesis. But no, their mouths are preoccupied with perpetual growth slogans like "Drill, baby, drill!"

But just for the sake of argument, let's say we can wave a magic wand or a hypnosis gismo and have ever-growing value without the use of more energy and materials. Suddenly bread tastes better, suits look spiffier...even hymns sound holier. All without using more energy or material. It's all in the mind, you see.

So, we spend more on it? Thus increasing GDP?

Prove it.

While the Worstalls of the world are busy with an exercise in futility, the rest of us can think about something more evident. Where does the money come from to spend on things of value? As Adam Smith noted in *The Wealth of Nations*, money originates when there is agricultural and extractive surplus. With agricultural surplus, not everyone has to farm. That frees the hands for the division of labor and the generation of real money to be spent on a variety of goods and services. Agricultural surplus is the physical basis of money and market expenditures.

Oh, sure, we can double the supply of money overnight if we really want to. If we all wake up one morning insisting that we value everything twice as much, why not double the money supply to account for it? But that's not growth in real GDP. It's mental and monetary only. The mental part is fine—a nice mood at the least—but the monetary part is called inflation!

The foundation of the real human economy is the producers. Only with surplus production will there be expenditures on consumption. Growing GDP takes more surplus production. Such are the trophic origins of money, in ecological terms. But as Worstall said, "When extremely bright people step off their own knowledge base, they can make very interesting mistakes when they attempt to explore other fields." I don't know if Worstall is extremely bright or not, but he obviously isn't conversant with ecology (also known as the economy of nature). That sets him up poorly for economic matters. If you don't get the basics of the real sector, you can make a real mess of the monetary sector.

If anyone still views this as an argument, maybe we can settle it democratically. After all, it seems that plenty of folks value democracy, so the more democratic the approach, the more valuable it should be (within limits, I'd say). So, let's take a vote. What do readers think is more feasible: ever-growing satisfaction and ever-growing GDP with no additional stuff? Or declining satisfaction and declining GDP as the supply of stuff declines?

I'd like to hear your thoughts. I do value your opinion. But whether you give it or not, I won't be spending a dime on it. GDP will just have to sit there.

References

Worstall, T. 2012. Economic growth will boil the planet in 400 years: or, what Tom Murphy the physicist needs to know about economics. *Forbes*, April 12, 2012.

Five Myths about Economic Growth

Myth #1. It's economic.

To be economic, something has to be worth more than it costs. *Economic* activity, per se, is more beneficial than detrimental. Technically speaking, "marginal utility is greater than marginal disutility."

If you liked a rug but liked your grandkids more, it wouldn't be smart to grab the rug out from under the grandkids. That's basic microeconomics. Yet if we look around and reflect a bit, doesn't it seem like all that economic activity is pulling the Big Rug out from the grandkids at large? Water shortages, pollution, climate change, noise, congestion, endangered species...there's no magic carpet in the offing for posterity.

Growth was probably economic for much of human history. But we have to know when times have changed and earlier policy goals are outdated. In the 21st century, when we're mining tar sands, fracking far and wide, and pouring crude oil by the ton into the world's finest fisheries, trying to grow the economy even further is looking like a fool's errand. That's basic macroeconomics.

Myth #2. Economic growth is often miraculous.

Right now, we've got the Chinese miracle. We're supposed to be on the cusp of an Indian miracle. Seems like we already had a more general Asian miracle, having to do with "tigers."

We've had Brazilian, Italian, Greek (yes Greek), Spanish, and Nordic miracles. There's been the Taiwan miracle, the miracle of Chile, and even the Massachusetts miracle. Don't forget the earlier Japanese miracle and more than one historic German miracle.

Let's hope these aren't the kinds of miracles they use to determine sainthood. Saint Dukakis, anyone?

No, economic growth was never, anywhere, a "miracle." It's never been more than increasing production and consumption of goods and services in the aggregate. It entails an increasing human population or per capita consumption; these go hand in hand in a growing economy. It's measured with GDP.

Whoop-de-do, right? Maybe Wall Street investors and journalists are an excitable lot, and it's easy enough to be surprised by a growth rate, but "miracle"?

Myth #3. Growth isn't a problem for the environment because we're dematerializing the economy.

Now *that* would be a miracle.

Let's get one thing straight: the economy is all about materials. "Goods," in other words. Oh, sure, services matter too. But the vast majority of services are for purposes of procuring, managing, or enjoying our goods.

The biggest service sector, transportation, is responsible for enormous environmental (and social) impacts. Transportation is instructive, too, about the relationship between goods and services. People don't line up at cash registers demanding random acts of transportation. No, it's all about moving materials—goods or people—from point A to point B and moving them economically. Every form of transportation takes energy as well as copious supplies of materials (for vehicles and infrastructure) and space.

With all the talk of "de-materializing," surely there must be services that transcend the physical, right? What about the Information Economy?

Myth #4. The human economy went from hunting and gathering through agriculture and on to manufacturing, and finally to the Information Economy.

Don't forget our lesson from the transportation sector: no transportation for transportation's sake. In the "Information Economy," what's all that information going to be used for? If it's not going to be used in activities such as agriculture and manufacturing (and transportation) how is it going to matter for economic growth?

The fact is, there never was—or always was—an information economy. Pleistocene hunters needed to read mammoth tracks more than we need to read our Twitter feed.

Now when it comes to processing information, the computer was more or less a "revolutionary" invention, like the internal combustion engine was for transportation. But what's less material about it? Just as today's hunters have semi-automatic rifles with high-power scopes, they have (material) computers that help them gather information for buying more (material) guns, scouting more (material) terrain and shooting more (material) deer. Anything about that seem greener than before?

Information has proliferated alright, in lock step with the material goods and services it's been used for. Yet to speak of the "Information Economy" seems like grabbing for some type of economic miracle, and we've all seen how cheap miracles are in economic rhetoric.

Myth #5. At least economic growth is egalitarian, because a rising tide lifts all boats.

Once upon a time, the rising tide metaphor may have had some merit. In the 21st century—think resource wars, climate change, endangered species—it's more like a rising tide flooding all houses. Which brings us back to Myth #1.

Bottom Line

It seems like all the talk of economic growth was overblown, more the result of Wall Street excitement and political rhetoric than sober thought. Maybe what we really want is economic slenderizing.

Economic Growth: The Missing Link in Environmental Journalism

Environmental journalists are like doctors. Doctors run from patient to patient, harried, dealing with symptoms more than causes. They're too busy dispensing pills to talk about holistic health. It's an approach that makes money for the health industry but isn't so great for public health.

Environmental journalists run from issue to issue, harried, dealing with environmental impacts more than causes. They're too busy dispensing stories to talk about context. It's an approach that makes money for the media but isn't so great for environmental protection.

The analogy isn't perfect. Environmental journalists don't have an obligation to protect the environment like doctors are obligated to patient health. But journalists are obligated to tell the truth: the truth, the whole truth, and nothing but the truth. Here we're concerned with the "whole" truth, and it's worth extending the analogy in this direction.

Let's say the doctor has an overweight patient. The patient was small as a child and developed an obsession with gaining weight. It's hard to shift mental gears. Fully mature now, this patient's top goal is growing even more! This has led to all kinds of problems: bad knees, high blood pressure, and sleep apnea to mention a few.

Now imagine the doctor prescribing more pills for each new ailment, never saying a thing about the patient's obsession with growth. When will the doctor talk about the big picture? The patient is just not getting it on his own. To him, getting even bigger seems like the solution to all problems, not the cause.

Similarly, we have a society—a readership—that considers economic growth the top priority. This unhealthy obsession has led to all kinds of problems: biodiversity loss, climate change, and ocean acidification to name a few. Yet the reader is just not making the connection. Growing GDP seems like the answer to all problems, not the cause.

A code of ethics prevents journalists from advocating policies. It's "just the facts ma'am." But environmental journalists would probably be working for the environment if they weren't writing about it. That's my guess after attending three of the last five Society of Environmental Journalists conferences.

Yet the journalists have been missing the environmental forest for the trees. Try to remember the last article you read about an environmental problem in which economic growth was even mentioned, much less explored with nuance. Can you?

Journalists covering climate negotiations sometimes identify economic growth as the goal in the way of progress. China and India aren't about to give up on growth now, and for that matter, neither is the USA. Our "way of life is not up for negotiation." But that's about it for coverage. There's little exploration of the nuances: of how in a 90-percent fossil-fueled economy, economic growth means climate change; of how "green" energy can't substitute for fossil fueling of the economy; of how a stabilized climate amounts to a steady state economy.

And that's just the context of one environmental problem—climate change. When, in reading about biodiversity loss, ocean acidification, depletion of aquifers, fisheries decline, etc., do we read about the linkage to economic growth? All environmental problems track with GDP growth, and it's no coincidence. The relationship between economic growth and environmental impact is causal, just as the connection between gaining weight and bad knees is causal. Economic growth is an 800-pound gorilla with two arms: population and per capita consumption. It doesn't happen without environmental impact.

It's ironic that environmental journalists don't tap into the big picture of economic growth. After all, generating a buzz is all about connecting with society's concerns. It's about relevance. What is more relevant today than economic growth? What is more covered in the broader media? What gets more attention from politicians?

The environmental journalist's take on economic growth will sound odd at first. Readers are used to thinking of economic growth as the solution to problems, not the cause. But that's OK. Readers are like the obese patient intent on gaining weight. When it dawns on them that economic growth is the cause of so many problems, not the solution, their interest will be piqued, and many will develop an appetite for journalism on economic growth and the sustainable alternative, the steady state economy. The whole truth will set them free from the fallacious rhetoric that "there is no conflict between growing the economy and protecting the environment."

Environmental journalists don't have an obligation to environmental protection. But they do have a unique opportunity. They have the opportunity to raise awareness of the whole truth, however inconvenient, that environmental protection doesn't square with economic growth.

Paul Krugman on Limits to Growth: Beware the Bathwater

Congratulations to Paul Krugman, whose *New York Times* opinion on "Slow Steaming and the Supposed Limits to Growth" hit the bullseye of at least one balloon. Landing at Washington-National the very day his opinion column appeared was like crashing back into the growth fetish of the American Fourth Estate. Out came the fresh air of an Australian balloon; back to the polluted, cynical rhetoric that "there is no conflict between growing the economy and protecting the environment."

Why the drama with Krugman's column? Partly due to uncanny timing; partly due to the stark juxtaposition of opinions. Having delivered the keynote address—on limits to growth no less—at the Australian Academy of Science's annual conference on environmental science, it struck me that decades of careful research could be undermined by the presumptuous pen of a well-placed economist. Something is wrong with that picture.

But only for so long, because those of us who recognize limits to growth have sound science, common sense, and burgeoning evidence on our side. The same cannot be said for Krugman's opinion.

Krugman got off to a shaky start with the very title of his column. No matter what he could say about "slow steaming," this was bound to be an article wrong-headed in using one sector (shipping) for drawing broad conclusions about a macroeconomic issue (economic growth). To extend a conclusion from the part to the whole is to commit the fallacy of composition. In this case, it's a bit like Krugman saying, "Your fingernails keep growing; why not the rest of you too?"

The mistake is common and destructive. When this mistake is made by a highly acclaimed economist in a widely-read opinion, the potential for destruction is multiplied. Politicians hide behind such Polyannaish opinions to pull out all the stops—fiscal and monetary—for economic growth. The casualties include not only environmental protection but the future economy and ultimately national security.

Next, in Krugman's lead-in paragraph he laments the "unholy alliance on behalf of the proposition that reducing greenhouse gas emissions is incompatible with growing real GDP" (Krugman 2014). Already we have two more problems. First, the argument alluded to in the title—that is, refuting limits to growth—is reduced to refuting just one negative impact of growth (i.e., climate change). What about all the other impacts and limitations of economic growth: liquidation of natural resources, pollution at large, habitat loss, biodiversity decline, and social side effects such as noise, congestion, and stress?

Second, in a maxed-out, over-stimulated, 90 percent fossil-fueled economy, Krugman wants us to believe we can grow the economy even more while reducing greenhouse gas emissions. No need to worry about little trends such as tar-sands mining in Canada, coal mining in China, and fracking in the USA. Slower steaming will save the day on climate change, and presumably for the rest of the planetary ecosystem.

Let's not let Krugman delude us. "Growing real GDP" isn't about an efficiency gain here and there. It means increasing production and consumption of goods and services *in the aggregate*. It entails a growing human population and/or per capita consumption. It means growing the whole, integrated economy: agriculture, extraction, manufacturing, services, and infrastructure. From the tailpipe of all this activity comes pollution.

Krugman seems to have fallen for the pixie dust of "dematerializing" and "green growth" in the "Information Economy." He may want to revisit Chapter 4 of *The Wealth of Nations*, where Adam Smith pointed out that agricultural surplus is what frees the hands for the division of labor. In Smith's day that included the likes of candle-making and pin manufacturing. Today it includes everything from auto-making to information processing, but the fundamentals haven't changed. No agricultural surplus, no economic growth. And agriculture is hardly a low-energy sector.

Adam Smith was among the great, classical economists who readily recognized limits to growth, all the way until at least John Stuart Mill. After that and throughout the 20th century, things got murky for economists as they turned increasingly to microeconomics, losing the forest for the trees. Mr. Krugman appears to be yet another victim of the "neoclassical" evolution of economics. Look to him for insightful opinions on banking regulations, fiscal politics, and other such topics that fit naturally under the rubric of an economics columnist. These are his babies, but beware the bathwater. Take his opinion on limits to growth at your peril, and that of your grandkids.

References

Krugman, P. 2014. Slow steaming and the supposed limits to growth. *The New York Times*, Opinion, October 7, 2014.

George Will, Doomsday, and the Straw-Man Sighting

A funny thing happened on the way to this column. Right when I was ready to accuse *Washington Post* columnist George Will of building another straw man to tear apart, one of Will's straw men appeared! It's as if Will himself cued it up, as I'll describe in a bit.

Meanwhile don't get me wrong. Will isn't right about a lot. He has long been loose with the facts on environmental issues, denying the causes and effects of resource scarcity, pollution, and climate change. His vision of perpetual economic growth is neoclassical naiveté. He displayed it again with "Calls for doomsday remain unheeded."

Will stubbornly remains a fawning fan of the late perpetual growther Julian Simon. No one likes to criticize the deceased, and Will counts on this and other social conventions to protect himself from critique. (Recently he hid behind society's respect for Native American tribes to shoot at federal government clean-air efforts.) But it's not a fair tactic, I'm not falling for it, and Simon was no saint anyway. Simon's culminating book (*The Ultimate Resource 2*) was the shoddiest semblance of "scholarship" I've ever seen, as I described at length in *Shoveling Fuel for a Runaway Train*. For Will to stick with Simon after all this time is a red flag over the teeny terrain of his scientific credentials.

Will has even been sucked into the junk-science vortex of Bjørn Lomborg, Simon's disciple and darling of pro-growth propagandists like the Competitive Enterprise Institute. Will thinks "potential U.S. gas resources have doubled in the last six years,"[1] as if even potential (not just

---

[1] https://tinyurl.com/sa6ygur, last viewed on 11/20/2019

economic) gas resources change with technology! No stranger to bad facts, Will says, "One of [Paul] Ehrlich's advisers, John Holdren, is President Barack Obama's science adviser." In reality it was the other way around: Ehrlich was Holdren's adviser. In other words, Will uses a mistaken claim to unleash a twice-removed, guilt-by-association attack, all in one sentence!

Despite the fact that Will has the combined credibility of Barry Bonds and BP Oil on environmental and sustainability affairs, there are reasons for empathizing with him at times. In fact, one reason plopped in my inbox this morning! The sender, a sustainability activist, first quoted from a web page of the Center for the Advancement of the Steady State Economy, "The CASSE position calls for a desirable solution—a steady state economy with stabilized population and consumption—beginning in the wealthiest nations and not with extremist tactics." Then he went on to complain:

"Unfortunately, there is no 'desirable solution'—I wish there were... Industrialism is by its very nature a temporary phenomenon; in the process of perpetuating it we consume the natural resources—primarily finite, non-replenishing, and increasingly scarce NRRs—that enable it. Unfortunately, the chickens are coming home to roost now—instead of 1,000 years from now—and there's nothing that we as a species can or will do about it, except suffer the inevitable consequences."

So, when George Will talks pejoratively about "calls for doomsday," he's got that one legitimate point, at least. For someone (a sustainability activist no less) to claim there is no desirable solution to the problem of uneconomic growth is defeatist at best, and patently false besides. Just because a solution—such as a steady state economy running at optimal size—is difficult to achieve does not mean it is out of the question or undesirable. What we should all agree on is that perpetual growth is out of the question, and then strive for the best alternative, handling the growing pains (or in this case, the de-growing pains) along the way.

Next, to paint "industrialism" with such a broad brush that it cannot be sustained, period, is another target on the straw man's back. We should expect Mr. Will to hit that bullseye every time. First of all, de-industrial-izing is no panacea; it's easy to envision an unsustainable, non-industrial economy hell-bent on growth. More to the point, who is to say we cannot sustain some industrial capital and production, especially with the use of renewable resources (picture a sawmill running on hydropower), for such a very long time that no one would consider it unsustainable. The problem is perpetual *growth*—always expanding the capital base and trying to produce more—regardless of the mechanical means by which that growth occurs.

And then, to top it off with, "there's nothing that we as a species can or will do about it, except suffer the inevitable consequences" almost makes me wonder who is farther from the truth: Will or the sustainability activist. After all, the activist is either not doing anything "about it" or considers himself too exceptional to be part of the human species. But I don't, and CASSE doesn't. We *are* trying to do something about it. That is, we're advancing the steady state economy—a desirable solution—instead of sitting on our doomed derrières while lamenting the forces of "industrialism."

I never thought I'd agree with George Will on a matter of sustainability, but I'll admit one thing: The caricatures he constructs are not always comprised of straw. Doomsday straw does exist but, unfortunately, some sustainability activists wear it too well.

BP: Beyond Probabilities

As much as I intended to cover the pending designation of GNP National Monument in Montana (where the glaciers at outdated "Glacier National Park" are melting as a monument to economic growth), that will have to wait until next time. This week, there's just no way a *Daly News* contributor could fail to focus on British Petroleum and the Deepwater spill.

Punctuated environmental disasters like Bhopal, Chernobyl, and Deepwater have a lot in common with ongoing, insidious disasters such as climate change, biodiversity loss, and pollution in general. The insidious disasters are so tightly linked to economic growth you couldn't separate them with a BP "top-kill" pump. But so are the punctuated disasters. And, as with the insidious disasters, the linkage of punctuated disasters to economic growth is never pointed out in the mainstream media.

The connection has to be pointed out, with emphasis and often, or we can forget about economic policy reform toward a steady state economy. Instead, naïve (or unscrupulous) politicians and economists will call for more economic growth in order to fund all the hapless responses such as hair booms, deepwater robots, and top-kills.

The linkage between economic growth and environmental disaster probably seems obvious or at least intuitive to people such as our CASSE signatories, but we've learned that it is far from obvious to many economists, businessmen, politicians, and others who haven't thought about it in these terms. So, let's think about it a bit...

Environmental accidents include a long, long list of leaks, spills, collapses, collisions, breaks, explosions, fires, derailments, and other wrecks and mishaps to match the variety of economic endeavors from which they stem. Here we are focused on accidents in the energy sector for two reasons. First, these accidents tend to be some of the most disastrous. Second, they are the most inevitable.

The first point is fairly obvious; the second point bears elaboration. Why are energy sector accidents most inevitable?

While economic growth may not absolutely require, say, diamond mining with all its environmental and social costs, economic growth absolutely requires more energy. Diamond mining may be an optional sector in a growing economy; the energy sector is not. Such is the trophic structure of the economy.

So, economic activity requires energy, and a growing economy requires more energy. Next, it doesn't take a rocket scientist to understand that the probabilities of energy sector accidents increase with—you got it—the level of activity in the energy sector! And gambling with the energy sector is no Saturday jaunt to the tribal casino, where you might hit the jackpot and make an escape. We're talking about national and global economies—tens of thousands of oil wells, thousands of coal mines, hundreds of nuclear plants, etc.—operating 24/7 and into the long run.

That means the "probabilities" play out!

In other words, it's not a matter of whether disasters will occur. And there's no question they will devastate ecosystems, blow by blow (they're disasters, remember?). At this point, we're BP: Beyond Probabilities. For all practical and policy purposes, disasters and devastation are certain. The only issue is how many disasters and how much devastation. These amounts are certainly a function of economic growth.

So, when they ask for ideas on what can be done about Deepwater or future such disasters, tell them to think of the big picture for a change and realize there's just no technofix to the probabilities playing out. The only real way to lessen the damage our grandkids will inherit is to start putting the brakes on this runaway economy we're driving. That entails macroeconomic policy reform, not technofixes, and consumer care, not consumer "confidence."

A steady state economy, even at the current dangerous size, would probably be the single greatest thing this generation could accomplish. The next generation may have to work on putting the economy in reverse for a while, until it fits within the planet's capacity for disasters. We need to lower the level of economic activity, starting with the energy sector, because in the long run, probabilities play out.

Who Moved My "Conservative"?

L ately folks have been asking, "Who moved my cheese?" Now it may be a cheesy way of putting it, but I haven't appreciated the moving of my "conservative." Not that I had one locked in the basement or mounted on the wall. No, it's the word itself that got moved. "Conservative" got uprooted from the fertile soil of sound linguistics and replanted in the political forests of Gobbledygook.

Of course, *Who Moved My Cheese* was all about change, and cheese gets moved all the time, so perhaps the moving of "conservative" is no big deal either. Yet I think it is. After all, in American politics there are but two major camps: liberals and conservatives. To slop around with words such as "conservative" or "liberal" is like slurring the words "I do" at a wedding. When you're at the altar, it is crucial to know: Do you or don't you? Everyone from the fiancé to the county clerk needs a meaningful answer.

In American politics, we need to know what "conservative" stands for. ("Liberal," too, but that's for another day.)

The problem here goes right to the core of the word. The core of the word, it bears emphasizing, is "conserve." This is not some veiled or irrelevant core. It's not like the "andro" in "android." The fact that "andro" means male is pure trivia, and you'll hardly use the word to begin with. Nor is "conserve" tucked into "conservative" like some Latin syllable in the genus *Parelaphostrongylus* (brainworm, if you must know). No, the "conserve" in "conservative" is there for all to see, dominating the word in letters, action, and emphasis.

According to the *Merriam-Webster Dictionary*, "conserve" means "to keep in a safe or sound state... *especially*: to avoid wasteful or destructive use." The first example given? To "conserve natural resources." Obviously! "Conserve" goes with natural resources like "defend" goes with country and "safeguard" goes with Constitution. That's why those who conserve natural resources are called "conservationists." (At CASSE, we like to call them "steady staters.")

The political manifestation of a conservationist, then, would warrant the label "conservative." Anything politically "conservative" ought to refer, *especially*, to the conservation of natural resources. Certainly, the word "conservative" should never be used to refer to the non-conservation of natural resources.

Therefore, it really takes the cake, cheesecake even, that the word "conservative" has come to mean such an anti-environmental, pro-growth, transform-the-world-into-plastic agenda. It's always "conservatives" who want to roll back environmental protections. "Conservatives" push for drilling in the Arctic. "Conservatives" want to gut the Endangered Species Act. "Conservatives" don't want to limit greenhouse gas emissions. Hummer drivers and Yukon drivers like Glenn Beck call themselves "conservatives."

"Conservatives" my keister!

Moving our cheese is one thing, but commandeering it and polluting it in such a way that we wouldn't want to use it again...that has to be some kind of sin. It's stealing, lying, and adulterating the truth, all in one. It's the killing of common sense, the death of candid dialogue. It's hiding a sow's ear in a silk purse.

Well, I can't rectify decades of rhetorical sabotage in one posting, but let me just clarify what it really means to be conservative, or at least what it's really supposed to mean. In a world of plain-spoken truth, I am conservative, and my friends are conservative. We're steady staters; we conserve natural resources. We ride our bikes to work, sometimes drive the hybrid (or some smallish car), and always shut the lights off. We vote for steady statesmen who are strong on conserving natural resources. We volunteer for organizations that help protect the environment, which amounts to conserving natural resources.

That's the real cheese, back where it belongs.

Who Moved Obama's Win-Win Cheese?

Whether or not you like President Obama or his policy preferences, you have to acknowledge his consistency. Even those with "zero regard" for the president confess, "At least Obama is consistent." But not consistently. There is one issue, at least, on which he hasn't held still, moving in and out like an octopus in a sunken ship. That issue is the relationship between economic growth and environmental protection. Based on his state of the union address, his current [2015] tack is a mixture of avoidance and vague allusion.

Yet Obama's inconsistency on this issue is nothing to be hypercritical of. In fact, given this recent turn, we might even say, "At least Obama is inconsistent." As odd as that may sound, it's better to be inconsistent when you were, at one time, dangerously wrong.

Obama's rhetoric on the issue has basically been through three phases, which can be categorized and paraphrased as:

- Integrity phase. "Economic growth is ultimately not sustainable, and that's becoming more apparent. We need a new economic model that protects the environment, like a steady state economy." This was the pre-presidential, relatively innocent phase, a distinctive feature of the original Obamanomics.
- Win-win phase. "There is no conflict between growing the economy and protecting the environment." Obama ventured onto this slippery slope of win-win rhetoric during the run-up to his re-election.
- Avoidance phase. "Economic growth is my top priority, and let me

elaborate on that... (Oh and by the way, we also have to protect the planet.)" In the state of the union address, this notion of protecting the planet was limited to climate change mitigation, and even this was kept in a separate compartment from growing the economy. No more win-win, growth and environmental protection. In fact, Obama used the word "environment" exactly zero times.

The progression from Obamanomics to the win-win rhetoric, while cynical, was predictable, but what happened next? What caused the President to retreat from win-win, nearly all the way back to a position of environmental irrelevance? After all, win-win has held a central spot on the Politician Bingo card for as long as baby boomers and younger can remember. Furthermore, the shining example of win-win since the late 1980s has been the marriage of economic growth to environmental protection. The wedding of these opposites allowed presidential candidates, from left to right, to appeal to pro-growth and pro-environment interests simultaneously. It didn't matter that it was a scientifically fallacious shotgun wedding. It worked at the political altar.

So, what happened? Did Obama move his own win-win cheese, or did some speechwriter move it for him? It's not like we have a trail—say a money trail—that's easy to follow. With a lot of issues, it's easy to backtrack a politician from his or her mouth all the way back to Big Money. It might be Big Gun Money generating rhetoric like "a good guy with a gun in every school," or Big Tobacco Money puppeteering, "I believe tobacco is not addictive." No matter how wrong, such well-endowed rhetoric sticks around long after everybody understands how fallacious it is. Eventually, though, it either goes away or becomes an icon of ridicule.

Yet Obama's dropping of the win-win rhetoric is different, because there is no money to be had from doing so. Big Money, even its better side in the grant-awarding foundations, will have nothing to do with talk about stabilizing the size of the economy or even slowing the rate of growth. In fact, Little Money doesn't want much to do with it either. This explains the plethora of organizations promoting various notions of a "new" economy or a "green" economy without coming clean on the fundamental conflict between economic growth and environmental protection. They're all chasing the money to keep their boats afloat.

Will the ironies ever cease?

Yet there are two things—both extremely powerful—that clarify the fundamental conflict between economic growth and environmental protection, loud and clear. One is science; the other is common sense.

The science is sound and sufficient, but it's not like the libraries are overflowing with it because, again, there's little money available for such research. Therefore, this type of research—ecological macroeconomics we might call it—tends to be swamped out by Big-Monied, "neoclassical" economics with its fallacious theories of perpetual growth. But ecological macroeconomics is there for the reading: theoretical and empirical detail about the trade-off between economic growth and biodiversity conservation, a stable climate, and ecological integrity in general. And we know that Obama's science advisor, John Holdren, has a background in the environmental impacts of economic growth.

So, Obama's relinquishing of the win-win rhetoric probably stems from a mixture of scientific awareness, plain old common sense, and perhaps a sense of pride. Obama recognizes that, with a short two years of presidency remaining, his legacy is ever more on the line. It would be a shame to end up like President Clinton, for example who is haunted by the inconvenient irony of his own unmitigated and relentless win-win rhetoric that "there is no conflict between growing the economy and protecting the environment."

Whatever the explanation may be, let's hope Obama sticks with phase 3, or even comes full circle to phase 1, the more innocent Obamanomics with its recognition that economic growth is unsustainable and increasingly harmful in a century already slated for extinctions, climate change, water supply shocks and the like, all in proportion to our obsession with increasing production and consumption of goods and services in the aggregate, otherwise known as economic growth.

Let's also hope he starts using the word "environmet" again, prominently and eloquently. This is the 21st century: the environment should be a central feature when assessing and discussing the state of the union. Let's even hope Obama starts re-connecting the two issues—environment and economy—but this time so publics and policy makers on both sides of the aisle get used to dealing frankly with the trade-off. Only then can we hope for policies that protect the environment, sustain the economy, re-secure the United States, and help to stabilize the international community.

References

Leonhardt, D. 2008. Obamanomics. *The New York Times Magazine*, August 20, 2008.

Part III

Brent Blackwelder

Time to Stop Worshipping Economic Growth

There are physical limits to growth on a finite planet. In 1972, the Club of Rome issued their groundbreaking report—*Limits to Growth* (twelve million copies in thirty-seven languages). The authors predicted that by about 2030, our planet would feel a serious squeeze on natural resources, and they were right on target.

In 2009, the Stockholm Resilience Center introduced the concept of planetary boundaries to help the public envision the nature of the challenges posed by limits to growth and physical/biological boundaries. They defined nine boundaries critical to human existence that, if crossed, could generate abrupt or irreversible environmental changes.

The global economy must be viewed from a macro-perspective to realize that infringement of the planetary boundaries puts many life support ecosystems in jeopardy. Without functional ecosystems, the very survival of life forms as well as human institutions is put in doubt, including any economy. There is no economy on a dead planet!

These boundaries apply to the economy because the economy is a wholly owned subsidiary of the ecosystems that make life on earth possible. (Some understanding of ecology should be a prerequisite for an advanced degree in economics!) Scientists are concerned that we have already overstepped the boundaries on biogeochemical flows (nitrogen) and biosphere integrity (genetic biodiversity).

Today's global economy and the various regional and national economies regularly neglect planetary boundaries. Crossing a boundary is tantamount to crashing through a guardrail and plunging over a cliff. The blind encouragement of economic growth that does not respect these boundaries is setting up human civilizations for collapse. Two of the most harmful types of growth are *ruthless* and *futureless.*

Ruthless growth benefits a few at the top but does nothing for the middle class. One of the reasons that Bernie Sanders' presidential campaign has attracted larger and larger audiences is that he says the most crucial issue facing the United States is the gross discrepancy between the middle class and the billionaire class.

Futureless growth destroys resources, such as water, forests, fisheries, and farmland that will be needed by our children and grandchildren, and by wildlife. Futureless growth directly conflicts with common family values. We tell our children to save for the future rather than squander their money. We don't tell them to outspend their peers. We don't tell them to judge the quality of their lives based on material possessions and quarterly financial reports.

To remain within the nine planetary boundaries, nations must shed the fetish of economic growth and transition to a true-cost, steady state economy. Some of the critical transition steps include:

1. Replacing the GDP as a measure of well-being (lots of work has been done on coming up with an index of sustainable productivity).
2. Getting the Securities and Exchange Commission (SEC) to require corporations to disclose their pollution externalities (the SEC is not hopeless, as can be seen by its recent decision to require CEOs to publish their salaries along with those of the average workers at their companies).
3. Going to a four-day work week to secure fuller employment (this has happened in some European countries; Canadian economist Peter Victor emphasizes this crucial transition step).
4. "Dematerializing" the economy (in the sense that it's cheaper to repair an appliance than it is to buy a new one).
5. Identifying the areas in which the economy should grow, and those where it should shrink or degrow (e.g., the usage of fossil fuels must decline sharply, while roof-top solar power grows substantially).
6. Identifying the most heinous types of economic growth (most notably ruthless and futureless growth) and showing how their costs exceed their benefits.
7. Stabilizing population to keep humanity from further transgression of the nine boundaries.

There are about seven billion people on earth today, and forecasts indicate there will be nine billion by 2050. Already, almost one billion malnourished people are feeling the squeeze as they painfully bear testimony to the truth of what Malthus predicted two centuries ago. Key first steps to stabilizing population in a progressive way are:

1. Empowerment of women.
2. Requiring all foreign assistance to be designed so that women will be better off as a result.
3. Making contraceptives widely available.

Our global economy is treating the planet as if it were a business in a liquidation sale. Even environmental organizations—devoted to environmental protection—have been slow to acknowledge the major causes of environmental degradation, such as perverse economic incentives encouraging raw resource extraction and nonrenewable energy use. We need environmental leaders to speak out for a new, just, and true-cost economy and challenge the mindless embracing of ruthless and futureless growth. Environmental leaders should be driving the push toward refocusing economic thinking on the changes that we will have to make if we are going to move to a healthier economy that exists within planetary boundaries. Only if humanity stays within these nine boundaries can it continue to develop and thrive for generations to come.

Deceptionomics

This March, at the Environmental Film Festival in Washington, DC, I saw a documentary on the destruction of the Aral Sea in Kazakhstan, once the world's fourth-largest inland lake. Soviet planners and decision makers fifty years ago decided to divert the two main tributary rivers of the Aral to grow cotton. Starved of freshwater inflows, the Aral Sea has shrunk to half its original surface area and lost 75 percent of its volume.

The productive fishery was wiped out, salinity levels in the lake tripled, and the water has been poisoned with pesticides. I wondered what kind of deceptive economic calculations were used to justify destroying one of the natural wonders of the world.

I recently argued that today's global marketplace is characterized by cheater economics—a corporate welfare system that has no part in a sustainable, steady state economy. There's another type of economics that's also in wide use today. It's not quite as "in-your-face" as cheater economics, but it's just as harmful because of the way it distorts reality. Deceptionomics uses "fool-you" accounting to omit genuine costs and misrepresent the true benefits and costs of economic transactions.

Robert Trivers' new book *The Folly of the Fools* examines the role of self-deception in human life. The animal kingdom is full of examples of deception by both predator and prey. For example, over 100 varieties of insects look like innocent twigs but consume other types of insects that unsuspectingly come close. Trivers applies his analysis of self-deception to the economics profession. Economics, he contends, is not yet a science because it fails to ground itself in underlying knowledge, namely biology. He writes, "...when a science is a pretend science rather than the real thing, it falls into sloppy and biased systems for evaluating the truth...models of economic activity must inevitably be based on some notion of what an individual organism is up to. What are we trying to maximize" (Trivers 2011)?

Here economists play a shell game, he notes, as they tell us that people attempt to maximize "utility." However, when asked what constitutes utility, they reply, "Anything people wish to maximize." How's that for circular logic? Sometimes a person will try to maximize income, sometimes food, and sometimes sex over both food and income. So, now we need "preference functions" to sort out all the competing preferences in an attempt to maximize utility, but Trivers points out that economics by itself can provide no theory for how the organism is expected to rank variables."

Another big mistake by economists is the conflation of two senses of utility—the utility of your actions to yourself and the utility of your actions to others. Most economists view these two kinds of utility as being aligned. Trivers says that economists "often argue that individuals acting for personal utility will tend to benefit the group." Thus, they "tend to be blind to the possibility that unrestrained pursuit of personal utility can have disastrous effects on group benefit." Trivers observes that economists assume (contrary to direct experience and biological evidence) that "market forces will naturally constrain the cost of deception in social and economic systems." He notes with astonishment that "such is the detachment of this 'science' from reality that these contradictions arouse notice only when the entire world is hurtling into an economic depression based on corporate greed wedded to false economic theory" (Trivers 2011).

In a steady state economy, we would seek to minimize deceptive practices. We would not delude ourselves with the ruse that GDP captures the essence of well-being. Nor would we have separate moralities for business and community. We teach our kids not to squander their allowance and to save some for the future. In family and community settings, people care about the long term and consider what kind of world our children and grandchildren will live in. But in business circles, all attention is riveted on quarterly returns. Economists employ a discount rate in their calculations that values the future 100 years from now as being worth almost nothing.

The truly deceptive nature of our current economic system can be seen by looking at the big debate over oil prices and the attempt to blame President Obama for the high price of gasoline. Meanwhile candidate Newt Gingrich proclaims on national TV that he has a plan for $2.50-a-gallon gasoline. But even at $4.00 per gallon, the price of gasoline is deceptively low.

Every day the USA is spending approximately $2 billion buying gasoline. What is remarkable and not disclosed to the public, writes Amory Lovins in his new article in *Foreign Affairs*, is the $4 billion in losses stemming "from the macroeconomic costs of oil dependence, the microeconomic costs of oil price volatility, and the cost of having our military forces ready for intervention in the Persian Gulf" (Lovins 2012).

The International Center for Technology Assessment reported in 2001 on the deception involved in the price of gasoline. It found that the real cost of gasoline, when the crucial indirect or hidden costs are included, was between nine dollars and fifteen dollars higher than the price paid at the pump.

Such estimates rarely appear in the mainstream media. As a result, many people are unaware of the high environmental and social costs of our economic transactions. Even if we remain unaware of these costs, we still have to pay for them. We'd be better off eliminating the deception embedded in our institutions and making economic decisions based on knowledge of true costs including the environmental impacts of growth. As long as deceptionomics rules, fuzzy math will be used to justify incessant GDP growth, and one by one we must say goodbye to the Aral Seas of the world.

References

Trivers, R. 2011. *The Folly of Fools: The Logic of Deceit and Self-Deception in Human Life*. Basic Books, New York.

Lovins, A. 2012. A farewell to fossil fuels: answering the energy challenge. *Foreign Affairs* 91(2).

Food and Agriculture in a
Steady State Economy

T he annual book festival of the Library of Congress just featured
Jonathan Safran Foer who spoke about his book *Eating Animals*.
He writes about his Jewish grandmother who survived World War
II on the run from Nazis, scavenging from garbage cans and always on the
verge of starvation. However, she refused to eat a piece of pork given her
by a kindly farmer because "if nothing matters, nothing is worth saving."

Foer's grandmother might cause us to wonder about the nature of production in a steady state economy. What would people eat and how would
it be grown? Would everyone be a vegetarian or vegan? Would genetically
engineered food be prominent? What about farm subsidies and the role
of biofuels? How many of the current agricultural practices in the USA
would even continue?

Since sustainable scale is the most important feature of a steady state
economy, the first issue to investigate is how environmental systems are
responding to agricultural practices—in particular, the effects of agricultural practices on climate. There is growing evidence that animal agriculture
is the number one cause of global climate destabilization, contributing more
to climate change than all of global transport put together. The late World
Bank ecologist Robert Goodland produced an analysis showing that at least
half of the human-caused greenhouse gases come from the production of
domesticated animals. Livestock and their byproducts account for over
32.5 billion tons of carbon dioxide a year, or roughly 51 percent of annual
worldwide greenhouse gases.

Here is the unsettling irony: factory farm-dominated agriculture, as a major climate destabilizer, is creating long-term weather changes that compromise the ability of the earth to produce food.

Plant ecologists estimate that for every 1-degree Celsius temperature increase, grain yields drop 10 percent. Climate disruption has led to serious melting of snowpacks and glaciers in most places. In the western USA, where snowpacks store about 75 percent of the water supply, the Natural Resources Defense Council reports that climate change could reduce this to 40 percent by 2060. Similar concerns exist for the great Asian rivers like the Ganges and the Mekong that originate in the Tibetan plateau.

These impacts are not being imposed on a planet with soils and grasslands in wonderful condition, nor with cautiously maintained stocks of groundwater. It's not a planet with a stabilized human population, either, but rather a population likely to reach 9–11 billion by 2050.

In contrast to this grim picture of the agricultural capacity of the planet, many encouraging trends in food production are emerging. Examples include growth of organic food consumption, expansion of farmers markets, the local food movement, the slow food movement, the food-miles movement, and initiatives to get healthy food into schools—all of which are heading in promising directions.

A steady state economy would be even more conducive to these trends. It would move away from control of food by transnational corporations and toward an increased number and diversity of small and medium-sized farms and healthy rural communities. Revamped agricultural systems would provide many varieties of food in ways that conserve soil and water and maintain long-term fertility of the land.

These promising developments are taking place not because of but in spite of the U.S. Department of Agriculture, which has, for the most part, been a giant promoter of animal slum operations and presider over the demise of the family farm.

Over ten million animals are slaughtered for food each year in the USA in factory slum operations that produce over 95 percent of the nation's meat. It is abundantly clear that meat-dominated megafarm agriculture is not sustainable (even from the climate/energy standpoint alone), and it could not be part of the food system in a steady state economy.

A steady state economy would not abide perverse subsidies as a cornerstone of agriculture. Conversely in the growth-obsessed USA, a curious mathematical formula governs the dispensing of Farm Bill subsidies: the more environmentally damaging and harmful to public health the practice or project, the larger the state and federal handouts.

Elect More Women: Prerequisite for a Sustainable Economy

In 1990 there were only two women in the U.S. Senate, but in 2013, 20 women will be serving in the Senate, and another 81 women will take office in the House of Representatives. With this record number of Congressional seats held by women, the USA is closing in on the global average (20 percent) for lawmaking bodies. [Editor's note: By 2019, 126 women (24 percent) were in the U.S. Congress.] This is good news because evidence suggests that governmental bodies with more women are more likely to tackle issues of social justice and environmental health.

Especially noteworthy in the 2012 elections were the defeats in the Missouri and Indiana Senate races where Todd Akin and Richard Mourdock (respectively) gained notoriety when they expounded their views on rape. Akin announced that in cases of "legitimate" rape, a woman's body had defenses to avoid pregnancy, and Mourdock asserted that a pregnancy from rape was something that "God intended."

It's worth celebrating USA electoral gains for women, but there is a long, long way to go. Iceland, for example, has a majority of women filling its university professor positions, and women comprise almost half the members of parliament.

Why is it so important to elect more women to positions of power? And is having 20 percent of seats enough to make a difference? Researchers Tali Mendelberg and Christopher Karpowitz found that when women make up 20 percent of a decision-making body that operates by majority rule, the average woman used only 60 percent of the floor time in comparison of what the average man used. But once women comprise 60 to 80 pecent of such a group, "they spoke as much as men, raised the needs of the vulnerable, and argued for redistribution" (Mendleberg & Karpowitz 2012).

Mendelberg and Karpowitz conclude: "When there are more women in legislatures, city councils and school boards, they speak more and voice the needs of the poor, the vulnerable, children and families—and men listen. At a time of soaring inequality, electing vastly more women might be the best hope for addressing the needs of the 99 percent" (Mendelberg & Karpowitz 2012).

Empowerment of women is crucial to any strategy for achieving a sustainable, steady state economy. Among the many reasons for this claim is the overarching problem of a growing population. The inexorable momentum of global population growth has led to over seven billion people on the earth today, with 360,000 births each day as opposed to 152,000 deaths.

At dinner tonight on this planet will be over 200,000 mouths to feed that weren't at the table yesterday. Such a figure should cause alarm because the quality of farmland on the planet is being significantly impaired by erosion, over-pumping of ground water, and the flood and drought cycles being exacerbated by global climate disruption.

Most experts on population growth observe that when women achieve a higher degree of status, respect, and power, they tend to have fewer children. Thus, empowerment of women is a key progressive strategy to stabilize population. In addition, slowing population growth could help reduce future climate-destabilizing emissions.

Another reason why the empowerment of woman is crucial pertains to government budget priorities. Lawmaking bodies dominated by men spend too much money on war and too little on conservation, protection, and restoration of vital ecosystems. If the majority of members of legislative bodies were women, budget priorities would be influenced by more discussion of environmentally sensitive economic policy.

So, let us consider two suggestions for continuing the trend of empowering women. The first is to enact a law that mandates a gender analysis before deploying USA foreign assistance in the form of projects, loans, or grants.

It surprises some people to hear that USA foreign assistance may be making women worse off. Most aid worldwide is not accompanied by any gender analysis that would answer the basic question: Will women be better or worse off as a result of this grant, loan, or matching fund? The nonprofit organization Gender Action offers information and resources for tracking the effects of international financial flows on women.

The second suggestion is to conduct more robust campaigns to fund family planning services worldwide, because the difference between a world reaching a population of 8 billion people in 2050 as opposed to 9.2 billion is hugely consequential. For example, a world of eight billion would emit roughly two billion fewer tons of carbon—an amount that is equivalent to what would be saved by eliminating all deforestation. Yet Population Action International points out that 215 million women who want to avoid pregnancy lack access to contraception and family planning.

References

Mendelberg, T., and C.F. Karpowitz. 2012. More women, but not nearly enough. *The New York Times*, November 8, 2012.

The Next President's Inaugural Speech (If Only...)

Once upon a time, the United States was a global pioneer of democracy and justice. The founders of this great nation articulated a noble vision of inalienable rights—life, liberty, and the pursuit of happiness. Times have changed. We have emerged from this presidential campaign with an ignoble vision of alienating wrongs—venom, vitriol, and the pursuit of pettiness. The campaign, including my campaign, dodged the most important issue of our era: coming to grips with the ecological reality confronting life on this planet. Today I pledge to make our nation once again the leader in solving economic, environmental, and social crises.

We have built a global economy that refuses to recognize ecological limits to growth. Repeated financial collapses, mushrooming corruption, and rampant speculation have characterized the last 20 years. We will blaze a new trail over the next 20 years, and will take bold steps to confront the overgrown, failing global economy. Better late than never, we will face the issues of climate change and relentless population growth that we have avoided for political expedience.

Modern industrial nations, with the USA among the leaders, emit so much pollution that we have endangered the stability of Earth's climate and jeopardized the survival of over one quarter of the planet's species. Our global population of over seven billion needs access to goods and services for a reasonable quality of life, but almost a billion are already struggling to obtain the barest of necessities. Our civilization is using natural resources much faster than the earth can regenerate them. Scientists explain that we would need one and a half Earths to keep consuming at our current rate.

We can do better than this. Our challenge is to create a true-cost economy, a sustainable economy that gives everyone a fair chance. No more cheater economics and no more casino economics. We will put the cheaters in jail and close down the Wall Street casinos.

Just as importantly, we will challenge the zealous pursuit of economic growth as the solution to all problems. Much of our so-called "growth" has cost us far more than it has been worth. We have *ruthless growth* that benefits a few at the top but does nothing for most Americans. We have *futureless growth* that destroys resources, such as water and farmland, that will be needed by our children and grandchildren. Our economy should align with our family values.

We will fund family planning so that the 250 million women worldwide who want such services can get them. All U.S. foreign aid will be screened to ensure that women will be better off as a result of the assistance.

While America has been sleeping, other nations have taken up the mantle of leadership:

- Iceland has become the leader in empowering women; women hold the majority of jobs in university education and have nearly half the seats in parliament.
- Bhutan has become the leader in measuring progress; this small but progressive nation has committed itself to maximizing gross national happiness rather than gross national product.
- Costa Rica and Sweden are leading the way in climate stabilization by instituting carbon taxes.
- Germany, a nation with unexceptional wind and solar potential, has become the world's largest generator of electricity in both categories.
- Several European nations are taking the lead on jobs, shifting to shorter work weeks to relieve unemployment and enable citizens to spend time as they choose.

It's encouraging to see other nations stepping up, but the United States needs to get in the game. We can no longer stand still and watch other nations pass by on the way to a sustainable 21st century economy.

Instead of rehashing the vicious debate over the deficit, I will move to implement a Robin Hood tax of just one half of one percent on financial transactions. This simple and fair tax would yield billions of dollars in revenue and prevent Wall Street gamblers from playing with our money. We *can* have prosperity without ruthless growth.

We will adopt a four-day work week. Rat races don't have winners. We will share the work to be done in this great country, so that everyone can have a job. We will capitalize upon the high productivity of our workers with a time dividend—meaning more time spent with our families and less time spent at the office.

Instead of fighting wars over oil, our military will prevent wars by helping to engineer the transition to clean energy. The military is already far ahead of the public and politicians in recognizing the threat of climate disruption and other limits to growth. For example, the U.S. Army is working to get its bases off the fossil-fueled electric grid and onto renewable energy. We will accelerate efforts like these and apply them across the nation.

We have only to look at the history of our nation to find inspirational leadership. The USA led in stewardship of the land with the establishment of Yellowstone National Park, the world's first, in 1872. Faced with mounting pollution in the 1960s, we responded to the challenge. Congress—yes our U.S. Congress—launched the first Earth Day on April 22, 1970 and assumed global leadership in reducing pollution by passing clean air and water laws. Other countries replicated our laws.

Now, even though most citizens are aware of profound economic and environmental problems at home and abroad, we have to acknowledge that the United States has been a drag, not a leader and not even a good follower. Instead of excuses and gridlock, we will start taking responsibility for our actions. My administration will put aside pessimistic notions of what we *can't* do and focus on what we *can* do.

I am not proposing an unachievable agenda for the American people, but rather a solid, workable plan to build on our past triumphs and cooperate with today's leading countries, regions, cities, and towns that have begun the quest for an economy with a future. We will systematically transform the United States of America from the biggest consumer to the biggest conserver. We will take up the challenge of leadership so that we can once again pursue the noble vision of life, liberty, and the pursuit of happiness, all of which requires a healthy environment.

Part IV

Rob Dietz

Breathing Room Economics

W hen I graduated from college, I was trapped beneath a mountain of debt. I had no money in the bank, $25,000 worth of student loans, and an interesting but low-paying job doing research on economic and environmental policy. I'm sure many students today look at that $25,000 figure longingly, as they struggle with debts upwards of $100,000. But for me, the $25,000 was huge. After adding up rent, food, loan repayment, and other basic expenses, I didn't have any money left at the end of each month. It became obvious very quickly that I was stuck. I didn't have something that I truly desired: breathing room.

In order to reclaim some breathing room, I decided to make paying off my student loans a top priority. I worked hard, cut expenses to the bone, and put as much extra money as possible toward those loans. I paid them off in three years and found myself with that much desired and often elusive breathing room. How did I use it? I took an entire summer off from work and rode a tandem bicycle with my girlfriend (now wife) across the country—a trip that changed my life for the better, but that's a story for another day.

The search for breathing room drives much of what we do in the economy as households, businesses, and even government agencies. We have pursued economic growth as a policy to gain breathing room. But, paradoxically, economic growth is now using up the very breathing room that we've been chasing and hoping to save for the future.

Every person, perhaps even every living organism, is interested in a little bit of breathing room—a chance to live life away from the edge of the cliff.

In his book, *The Beak of the Finch*, Jonathan Weiner has written, "The lucky individual that finds a different seed, or nook, or niche, will fly up and out from beneath the Sisyphean rock of competition. It will tend to flourish and so will its descendants—that is, those that inherit the lucky character that had set it a little apart" (Weiner 1994:142).

Weiner's quote provides an eloquent evolutionary perspective on the benefit of establishing some breathing room. Nature imposes a lattice of limits upon life; there is only so much energy available, so many nonrenewable resources, and a fixed speed at which renewable resources can be regenerated. Figuring out how to secure some leeway within this lattice is a grand goal of all creatures, be they sunflower sprouts, chickadees, or human beings.

The story of human striving, whether considered in the context of an individual or an entire economy, features the quest for breathing room as a central theme. Attainment of breathing room bestows a greater level of security, a wider array of choices for how to spend time and allocate resources, and greater possibilities for meeting needs. Early economists such as Francois Quesnay and Adam Smith recognized the importance of breathing room in the form of agricultural surplus. It is precisely this agricultural surplus that allows for the division of labor. Without being occupied by hunting, gathering, growing, or otherwise obtaining sustenance, people can spend their time and energy on other productive activities. Division of labor, in turn, has generated efficiencies and economic growth that have, in the past, provided even greater quantities of breathing room.

Yet the emergence of breathing room in the economy has raised a question, not unlike the one I had when I paid off my student loans: What do we do with it? In the economy of a single household, this choice might take the form of purchasing more goods and services. It might also take the form of working fewer hours, spending more time on leisure activities, and sharing extra resources with family, friends, or community members.

What about the whole economy, then? An economy is essentially a very large household. (The word "economy" actually derives from the Greek word for household, *oikos*). A household contains a small number of people interacting with one another and consuming a quantity of goods and services. An economy is simply a larger number of people consuming a larger quantity of goods and services. The question of what to do with breathing room poses choices to households and the economy as a whole.

National, regional, and global economies are not sentient beings, however; they don't recognize and cogitate upon the range of breathing room choices. In the USA and many other countries, we tend to spend our breathing room the same way: in an unending and unsound cycle of economic growth. We use it to expand the scale of the economic enterprise; we plow it right back into growth, and then again we have to stare down the possibility of running out of air.

The cycle comprises these steps:

1. We grow the economy by increasing the production and consumption of goods and services, indicated by a growing GDP.
2. As the economy grows, it begins to bump up against ecological limits, and we experience the negative effects of that growth. Examples include excessive and unhealthy pollution, loss of natural resources, degradation of ecosystems, poverty, and famine.
3. We use technological innovation, which is intimately connected to economic growth, to push back the immediate limits to growth. The most stunning example is the Green Revolution, in which Norman Borlaug and colleagues developed a variety of farming techniques to increase agricultural output and world food supplies.
4. We establish breathing room. In the case of the Green Revolution, malnutrition, famines, and starvation were avoided.
5. We use our breathing room to go on growing the economy, and the cycle repeats itself. After the Green Revolution human population, production, and consumption continued their exponential upward march.

A critical change, however, occurs each time through the cycle. Ecological limits become more imposing, more ultimate, as the consequences of growth shift from the local to the global scale. Instead of worrying about a local river catching fire, we are now worried about destabilizing the climate of the entire planet. In turn, the technological innovation needed to deal with these consequences becomes more sweeping and complex. As population continues increasing, stocks of natural capital decline, and technological solutions require increasing complexity, the prospects of achieving lasting breathing room become more and more precarious.

Why, then, must we spend our breathing room on growth? What about short circuiting this cycle of growth? The economy is a human construct, and growth of the economy is not an ironclad natural law. It is a human choice, whether or not to grow the economy. Granted, our institutions and culture are geared for growth. Cessation of growth is avoided at all costs for fear of unemployment and social instability, but with growth working like a huge vacuum cleaner sucking up all our breathing room, perhaps we'd better get to work on changing our institutions and culture. With the right economic framework in place, we can take our breathing room and cut out steps one and two of the cycle. In a steady state economy, we can use our breathing room for innovation and development, rather than for growth.

Progress and prosperity are not about ever-increasing consumption of goods and services. True progress and real prosperity are about meeting needs, achieving a high quality of life for all people, and sustaining natural resources and useful infrastructure to provide opportunities for future generations. Breathing room is the main ingredient in the recipe for progress and prosperity. Unmindful pursuit of economic growth is eating up this main ingredient before we can even finish preheating the oven. Establishing a steady state economy, with stable population and stable throughput of energy and materials, is the way to protect our breathing room. The sooner we get started on the transition, the sooner we can all breathe a little easier.

References

Weiner, J. 1994. *The Beak of the Finch: A Story of Evolution in Our Time.* Vintage Books, New York.

Storage Nation

I t's hard to know where to begin a rant about the materialistic mess that our culture has made of Christmastime in the USA. An easy target is the Thanksgiving midnight-madness sales at big-box retail stores. And there's always those devious marketers who use nostalgia to turn December into a month of mass consumption. But there's one industry that, more than any other, epitomizes materialism and our seemingly limitless propensity to consume: self storage.

Self-storage businesses are warehouses where people rent garages to hold their excess stuff. In the not-too-distant past, a small number of self-storage businesses catered to homes in transition (such as when people were moving from one place to another). On the pop culture scene, if self storage made any appearance at all, it was in a macabre role. For instance, in the film *The Silence of the Lambs*, Clarice Starling searches a storage unit and finds a pickled head in a jar.

Oh, how things have changed! Over the past few decades self-storage facilities have popped up faster than Starbucks outlets. The USA has over 2.2 billion square feet (78 square miles) of rentable space, more than three times the size of Manhattan Island. One out of every ten American households now leases a unit.

What's going on here? Two separate currents have converged into a riptide that drags people out to the sea of self storage. The first current is the credit card-fueled shopping frenzy that has put many Americans in a position of owning too many possessions. The second current is the promotion of self storage as an investment opportunity for entrepreneurs.

The first current is pretty well documented, so let's float along with the second current for a bit.

The place to get started is a bookstore or your local library. There you might be able to find *How to Invest in Self-Storage, Self-Storage Investments,* or *Rent It Up! Four Steps to Unlocking the Profit Potential in Your Self-Storage Business.* If you prefer fiction, there's even a novel, *Self Storage.*

Here's a quote from the opening of *Rent It Up*: "But if you are trying to create as much profit as you can and build a sustainable business, as well as a real estate asset that will increase in value far faster than your competitors', then you are in the right place and should keep on reading" (Jordheim 2009:4).

It's not that easy to define the word "sustainable," but one wonders what meaning the author has when he refers to building a sustainable self-storage business.

One thing's certain about sustainability: it doesn't result from continuous GDP growth. The Self Storage Association (SSA), the trade organization and lobbying arm of the industry, reports that self storage is a $20 billion industry. It has been the "fastest growing segment of the commercial real estate industry over the last 30 years and has been considered by Wall Street analysts to be recession resistant based on its performance since the economic recession of September 2008."[1] What has made the industry recession-proof? One answer is that foreclosures encourage the newly homeless to move their stuff into temporary storage. In the age of uneconomic growth, including subprime mortgage crises, the self-storage industry appears to be a real leader!

Not everyone has the means to start a self-storage business, but would-be entrepreneurs have another way to get in the game. A cottage industry has developed around auctions from failures in self storage. When a tenant fails to make payments on a self-storage rental, the storage company can auction off the contents of the unit. Another trip to the bookstore or library can catch you up on this trend. These books explain how to exploit such a circumstance: *Making Money with Storage Auctions, How to Make Boxes of Cash with Self-Storage Auctions,* and *Mini Storage Auctions: Uncover the Cash Within.*

It's a surprise that no one has written *How to Make Money Writing and Selling Books about Self-Storage Auctions*!

Moving from the unreal to the surreal...self storage has rebounded from its lowly pop-culture status in *The Silence of the Lambs.* The cable channel A&E broadcasts a program called *Storage Wars* about people competing for

---

[1] https://www.selfstorage.org/LinkClick.aspx?fileticket=fJYAow6_AU0%3D&portalid=0, last viewed on 11/20/2019

profits in self-storage auctions. According to A&E's website, *Storage Wars* ranks as their top series of all time among adults aged 25-54. The series had 2.8 million viewers per episode and peaked at 3.8 million.

In the spirit of regaining a positive attitude during this holiday season, I'd like to propose a New Year's resolution for the nation. Let's ditch our storage units. It should be a snap for the third-most-popular type of self-storage customers: people storing items they no longer need or want. And for other customers, downsizing can be downright liberating. This Christmas season, the best gift of all is the gift of less-cluttered lives.

References

Jordheim, T. 2009. *Rent it Up! Four Steps to Unlocking the Profit Potential in Your Self-Storage Business*. Wheatmark, Tucson, AZ, USA.

Pulling Back the Curtain on Economic Growth's Magic Act

A good story often includes a touch of magic—just ask *Harry Potter* or *Twilight* fans. Now, see if you can spot the magic in the following passage by Charles Wheelan from his book *Naked Economics*, in which he considers the question, "Who feeds Paris?":

> Somehow the right amount of fresh tuna makes its way from a fishing fleet in the South Pacific to a restaurant on the Rue de Rivoli. A neighborhood fruit vendor has exactly what his customers want every morning—from coffee to fresh papayas—even though those products may come from ten or fifteen different countries. In short, a complex economy involves billions of transactions every day, the vast majority of which happen without any direct government involvement (Wheelan 2010: 4).

Let's ignore for now that Wheelan's "right amount" of fresh tuna corresponds to a disappearing fishery (and the closure of vast fishing areas in the South Pacific). Wheelan's argument and the main message of free marketeers seems to be that Twinkies sprout spontaneously on supermarket shelves. Hamburgers originate from the silver stovetops of McDonalds restaurants. Water itself flows from shiny taps, translucent bottles, and fancy vending machines. We don't need to concern ourselves with trifling matters such as where this stuff ultimately comes from or how it arrives. Because of the magic of the market, we only need to know how to get our hands on sufficient cash, credit, or public funds to buy the stuff.

To a neutral observer, it certainly can look like magic—like Adam Smith dressed as Merlin, summoning all this visible wealth with his invisible hand. That's essentially what Wheelan and other economic analysts are saying. Through the magic of free markets, we can produce and consume an ever-increasing amount of stuff (and as a side note, we'll be rich enough to clean up any associated environmental messes, or at least export them to less enlightened nations).

That's some trick, but it's not real magic—it's just an illusion. If we take a step back and observe what's happening, we can expose the illusion and see that the market has something up its sleeve: cheap energy. Pulling up that sleeve is the crowning achievement of a new book called *Energy: Overdevelopment and the Delusion of Endless Growth*, edited by Tom Butler. With photographs that manage to frighten and inspire at the same time, and with essays that provoke deep thought and deeper concern, the authors clarify how the economy is really able to achieve "miracles" such as the shipment of papayas to Paris, and it assesses the prospects for keeping the magic act going.

Every economic transaction is underwritten by a continuous supply of abundant and cheap energy, a supply that "supports the entire scaffolding of civilization" (Heinberg 2012:8). The complex web of trades and transactions and mass consumption have been made possible by the exploitation of energy-dense fossil fuels. And continued growth of such an economic system requires increasing supplies of energy.

Energy includes facts about the fossil-fueled economy that are well known in some circles but ignored in most. For example:

- One gallon of gasoline, which costs a few dollars, is so energy-dense that it can push a 3,000-pound vehicle twenty miles.
- If human labor were used to meet the energy requirements of a typical American lifestyle, more than a hundred people (dubbed "energy slaves") would have to work around the clock for each American.
- Since the dawn of the industrial revolution, energy use and economic activity have increased in lockstep.
- Fossil fuels are indeed depletable, and burning them produces serious environmental side effects.

These facts help illuminate the predicament of modern society. We've built a set of institutions and a way of life that practically require continuous economic growth. But such growth is entirely dependent on access to cheap energy, and using more and more cheap energy is digging us into a deeper and deeper hole of spoiled landscapes, unstable climate, and biodiversity loss. But politicians, pundits, and the public have swept this predicament under the rug with the insane assumption that economic growth can go on forever with technological ingenuity, global market efficiency, and labor productivity (all of which are dependent on access to cheap energy).

It can be a real downer to contemplate the way humanity has used so many energy resources—freely provided by nature—to dig this hole. But the authors of *Energy* refuse to wallow at the bottom of the hole. Instead, they construct a ladder with rungs made out of ideas for change—ideas like educating the public to develop widespread energy literacy, conserving energy resources and natural landscapes, and establishing resilient communities. These rungs offer a hopeful transition to better ways and better days. The hopeful conclusion is that we can figure out how to live the good life in a powered-down economy—an economy that accepts *enough* as its organizing principle rather than *more*.

In her sobering and contemplative afterword, Lisi Krall (2012:332) writes, "Perhaps the real question of progress is not how to forge a new energy frontier, but how to forge a different model of economic organization and purpose, a model that isn't predicated on never-ending growth and a belief that there are no real biophysical limits." She believes it's time to give the magicians the hook. Luckily Krall and her colleagues in ecological economics, along with the authors of *Energy*, have been working on an economic model that is based on scientific observation and humility rather than magical thinking and arrogance.

References

Butler, T, and G. Wuerther. 2012. *Energy: Overdevelopment and the Delusion of Endless Growth*. Watershed Media, Plymouth, MA, USA.

Heinberg, R. 2012. A Deeper Look at the Energy Picture. Page 8 *in* T. Butler and G. Wuerther, eds. *Energy: Overdevelopment and the Delusion of Endless Growth*. Watershed Media, Plymouth, MA, USA.

Krall, L. 2012. Afterword: Places where the wind carries the ashes of ancestors. Pages 331-334 *in* T. Butler and G. Wuerther, eds. *Energy: Overdevelopment and the Delusion of Endless Growth*. Watershed Media, Plymouth, MA, USA.

Wheelan, C. 2010. *Naked Economics*. W.W. Norton & Company, New York.

The Influence of Donella Meadows and *Limits to Growth*

"There are no limits to growth and human progress when men and women are free to follow their dreams."

This cornucopian quote sounds like something a Disney character would say, but it's actually chiseled in stone on a monument in the heart of Washington, DC. These are the words of Ronald Reagan, and they have a permanent home in the atrium of the government building that bears his name. These words also seem to have a permanent home in the economic strategy of the USA and just about every other nation.

Reagan's quote oozes with optimism. His confident attitude and his gift for inspiring people formed the core of his popular presidential style, even if his rhetoric sometimes strayed far from reality. In the quote above, Reagan cleverly equated growth (which he championed for political reasons without considering the long-term environmental and social implications) with human progress (which pretty much every voter can get behind).

One public figure rivaled Reagan's hopefulness and ability to inspire yet, unlike Reagan, advocated for environmental protection and human progress by exploring the *disadvantages* of economic growth. She was a humble writer and farmer but, first and foremost, she was a scientist who rooted her analyses in the laws of physics and ecology. When Donella Meadows passed away suddenly in 2001, humanity lost a leading light.

Once you start reading Meadows' *Global Citizen* columns, it's hard to stop before you've read the entire 16-year archive. With wit, style, and uncommon insight, she tackled some of the most pressing social and environmental problems, and her writing was so good that the column was nominated for a Pulitzer Prize. She became one of the most influential people to promote the vision of a sustainable society. In fact, the Post Growth Institute ranked her at number three (right behind E. F. Schumacher and Herman Daly) in their list of the top 100 sustainability thinkers.

Meadows became internationally famous in 1972 as the lead author of *The Limits to Growth*. She and her coauthors, Dennis Meadows, Jorgen Randers, and William Behrens combined principles from the emerging field of system dynamics with newly developed computer modeling capabilities to assess the implications of ongoing growth in population, food production, industrial output, pollution, and consumption of nonrenewable resources. It's hard to overstate the influence of *Limits*, which was translated into twenty-five languages and became the best-selling environmental book of all time. That's a stunning achievement on its own, but it's all the more impressive for a book that covers such a disconcerting topic by presenting a bunch of output from a computer model.

The book's level of influence can be demonstrated by three pieces of evidence beyond the sales figures. The first piece of evidence comes from the realm of politics. Jimmy Carter, a scientist and farmer like Meadows, was clearly inspired by her work and that of other like-minded scholars. (He even hosted E. F. Schumacher at the White House). In his 1979 "Crisis of Confidence" speech, Carter called for conservation of energy, sharing of resources, and pursuit of meaning through channels other than "owning things and consuming things." That sounds a lot like a practical and hopeful approach to dealing with the limits to growth. But Carter's political rivals re-branded his speech as the "Malaise Speech." They successfully undermined his message, which was seen as a threat to corporate power and unchecked economic growth.

The second piece of evidence is closely related to the backlash heaped on Carter, which helped sweep him out of office and set the stage for the era of reckless Reaganomics. *The Limits to Growth* received the same type of backlash as Carter. Big-money detractors took such strides to discredit the book that millions of people mistakenly believe it was debunked years ago. This is nonsense—the book's analysis and its underlying message have held up incredibly well.

In 2008 the Australian Commonwealth Scientific and Industrial Research Organization took a close look at the book's scenarios. Their findings showed that thirty years of historical data compared favorably to key features of the book's business-as-usual scenario (ominously, this scenario results in collapse of the global economic system sometime around 2050). The fact that *The Limits to Growth* struck such a nerve and raised the ire of so many critics serves as a potent reminder of its influence.

The third piece of evidence is anecdotal. I bought my own copy of *The Limits to Growth* (a 1975 second edition) from a used bookstore a few years ago. The book's original owner received it as a Christmas present from someone named Rex. In his "Merry Christmas" note on the inside cover, Rex wrote, "I haven't read this yet, but it's supposed to contain some interesting ideas on where we are heading."

Meadows and company summarized "where we are heading" right up front by stating these three far-reaching conclusions:

1. If the present growth trends in world population, industrialization, pollution, food production, and resource depletion continue unchanged, the limits to growth on this planet will be reached sometime within the next 100 years. The most probable result will be a rather sudden and uncontrollable decline in both population and industrial capacity.
2. It is possible to alter these growth trends and to establish a condition of ecological and economic stability that is sustainable far into the future. The state of global equilibrium could be designed so that the basic material needs of each person on earth are satisfied and each person has an equal opportunity to realize his individual human potential.
3. If the world's people decide to strive for this second outcome rather than the first, then the sooner they begin working to attain it, the greater their chances of success will be (Meadows, et al. 1972: 23-24).

Detractors of *The Limits to Growth* clearly had an agenda—they didn't want any obstacle to impede their quest for unlimited profits and accumulation of wealth. But Meadows and company had an agenda, too. Their agenda, revealed in the second concluding point, is profoundly humanitarian. They were desperate to find a way to maintain human well-being without undermining the life-supporting systems of the planet.

We've made disappointing progress on the third, concluding point of Meadows and company over the last forty years. Even so, their admonition still holds. The sooner we begin working toward a steady state economy, the greater our chances of providing a lasting prosperity for all of civilization.

References

Meadows, Donella, D.L. Meadows, J. Randers, and W.W. Behrens III. 1972. *The Limits to Growth*. Universe Books, New York.

Hooray for the Underdog

W hat's more compelling than an astonishing upset? We seem instinctively drawn to the underdog; we routinely root for the resilient scrapper who refuses to back down. It's why Team USA over the Soviet Union in the 1980 Olympics was memorialized as the Miracle on Ice. It's why we cheered when Rocky Balboa went toe to toe with Apollo Creed (and subsequently KO'd *All the President's Men*, *Network*, and *Taxi Driver* at the Oscars). It's why Harry Truman's defeat of Thomas Dewey in 1948 is one of the most famous U.S. presidential elections. And it's why David and Goliath is one of the most beloved biblical stories.

There are some powerful think tanks promoting "green" ideas around the world, especially when it comes to "green growth," green technology, and green jobs. In a stunner, CASSE prevailed over them all as it was named the Best Green Think Tank of 2011 by the sustainability gurus at TreeHugger. Despite a miniscule budget and a skeletal staff consisting almost entirely of dedicated volunteers, the Center for the Advancement of the Steady State Economy overcame odds almost as long as its name.

Perhaps it's not all that shocking of an upset after all. With each passing day, the public is becoming more skeptical of the status quo and more receptive to CASSE's message. Infinite economic growth on a finite planet makes no sense. CASSE's message is difficult to hear and internalize, especially amidst the constant clamor for evermore growth. But accepting this message is a prerequisite to making the transition to a steady state economy, and CASSE is the leading organization calling for this transition.

As TreeHugger notes, "When it comes down to advocating for what we humbly submit to readers as the single most important economic concept of the 21st century, CASSE comes out on top." And CASSE is in good company—awards are piling up for people and organizations daring to challenge the orthodoxy of perpetual economic growth:

- The New Economic Model, a project of NEF (the New Economics Foundation), has been named a 2011 semi-finalist in the Buckminster Fuller Challenge.
- The Post Carbon Institute won a DoGooder Nonprofit Video Award for its outstanding "300 Years of Fossil Fuels in 300 Seconds."
- Herman Daly won the Lifetime Achievement Award from the National Council for Science and the Environment.
- The Global Footprint Network won the Skoll Award for Social Entrepreneurship.

These awards help validate the messages being delivered by CASSE, NEF, the Post Carbon Institute, Global Footprint Network, and other organizations dealing proactively with limits to growth. They increase public awareness of noteworthy efforts, and provide inspiration for following leaders in the right direction. And, who doesn't enjoy an underdog victory?

Part V

James Magnus-Johnston

Are We Hard-Wired to Think We Can Grow Forever?

I f rational arguments were primary catalysts for social change, perhaps a steady state economy would already be a reality. Research in
behavioral economics and cognitive psychology is beginning to help
us understand why human beings don't always make decisions that are in
their best interests. Can we overcome our irrational, maladapted mental
hard wiring to thrive in a post-growth future?

Trailblazing behavioral economists like Daniel Kahneman have discovered
that human beings are highly irrational creatures prone to delusion,
cynicism, and short-termism. In ecological economics, Bill Rees has argued
that our mental genetic presets have hard-wired us for overconsumption
and ecological doom. The futurist Peter Seidel has summarized these
"sustainability shortcomings" of *Homo sapiens* in a series of fiction and
non-fiction books.

Adding to this body of literature is a new theory by Ajit Varki and Danny
Brower, who argue that these shortcomings stem from an overarching
psychological predisposition to denial. In sustainability matters, denial might
be characterized as the failure to accept the deleterious consequences of
economic growth in favor of accepting comfortable fictions that reinforce
the status quo. Head-scratching environmentalists often use the word
"denial" to reference the irrational "climate change deniers," who accept the
science pertaining to familiar things such as internal combustion engines,
modern appliances, or GDP growth, yet are dismissive of climate science
and planetary boundaries. Why are human beings so good at denial?

Ecological economist Bill Rees argues that our ancient triune brain is hard-wired for short-term rewards, and those rewards have been amplified by the abundance of our fossil fuel-driven economy. Our brain, which runs on an outdated OS, has constructed a myth of perpetual growth wherein we can grow the economy and achieve short-term rewards forever.

In *Denial: Self-Deception, False Beliefs, and the Origins of the Human Mind*, Varki and Brower take it one step further. The late Danny Brower asked Varki, a biologist, why other smart, self-aware animals such as elephants, apes, dolphins, whales, or magpies, have not achieved levels of intelligence seen in human beings. Many of these animals can recognize themselves, communicate with one another, and mourn relatives or companions. They have all had more time than *Homo sapiens* to evolve, too.

Put another way, what is most distinctive about human thinking? The theoretical, though as yet unverifiable, answer put forward by Varki and Brower revolves around two things. First, humans are aware of the thoughts of others. Second, humans have the ability to deny reality. In other words, denial is the essence—or a big part thereof—of what it means to be human! They argue that as human beings became aware of their mortality, some fell into depression while others were able to carry on without becoming crippled by this realization. Mind over reality became a defining characteristic, enabling us to maintain sanity in the face of danger. Those who suffer from depression are often more aware of reality, they note, which in turn can cause a crippling level of anxiety. Such anxiety can even cause an avoidance of procreation, leading to an evolutionary dead end.

But in the Anthropocene, have the tables turned? Now, reality-accepting behavior may be an evolutionary boon. Rather than leading to a dead end, accepting the reality of overconsumption and overpopulation may result in actions that increase the likelihood of human survival. Could it be that those who accept reality have suddenly become cultural (r)evolutionaries better adapted for long-term human survival? Can the shift happen quickly enough to improve our survival prospects?

Perhaps the very evolutionary mechanism that led to our propensity for denial may also temper our unfortunate inclinations. At the point when human beings developed a capacity for denial, we would have changed the "cultural software" emanating from our "mental hardware," which demonstrates that change is possible. We are, evidently, capable of changing the way we interact with reality (although the speed at which this may occur is anyone's guess).

Dr. Varki calls for us to temper our denial in order to avoid climate destabilization. Most types of denial, he says—about high national debt loads, eating too much red meat, smoking cigarettes, or refusing to wear seatbelts—aren't existential threats to the entire species. Climate destabilization, as with a nuclear holocaust, is a different matter. A shift towards reality-accepting behavior would help us see the merits of a steady state economy as a crucial policy goal.

References

Varki, A, and D. Brower. 2013. *Denial: Self-Deception, False Beliefs, and the Origins of the Human Mind*. Twelve, New York.

What About Innovating
Beyond the Growth Trap?

A new voice has emerged recently in Canada called the "Ecofiscal Commission," which could have the funding, clout, and determination to steer the country in a more promising direction. The group includes high-profile economists, former political leaders, and high-powered financiers. They define "ecofiscal policy" as something that "corrects market price signals to encourage the economic activities we do want (job creation, investment, and innovation) while reducing those we don't want (greenhouse gas emissions and the pollution of our land, air, and water)." There seems to be a semblance of steady-state thinking among this otherwise rather conventional lot.

Not so fast. The Ecofiscal Commission recently clarified that it "believes that our economies can continue to grow, even as we improve the environment by polluting less and using our natural resources more efficiently." I found it noteworthy that this group of high-profile individuals decided it was necessary to address the question of growth. Perhaps that's because folks like myself don't believe their policies are sufficient to address 21st century challenges, such as anthropogenic climate change and mass extinction.

One of their commission members, Dr. Dick Lipsey, is a "renowned expert in the field of economics and innovation," and Professor Emeritus of Simon Fraser's Department of Economics. In a recent Ecofiscal blog post[2], he rehearsed a standard narrative of innovation and technological

---

[1]https://www.resilience.org/stories/2013-12-24/political-analysis-energy-overdevelopment-and-the-delusion-of-endless-growth/, last viewed on 11/18/2019

progress that many ecological economists are familiar with. His narrative ignores rebound effects and fails to identify exactly what technologies will systematically reduce our material footprint. He even seems to suggest that if we don't grow the economy, our health outcomes will decline due to a lack of medical innovation.

He goes on to write about how those who "think only of today's commodities and today's technologies, do not see the possibilities of raising living standards, while also dealing with pollution, through technological advance." This seems straightforward enough—we don't know what we don't know. New technologies will emerge over time. He then proceeded to make a sweeping claim by listing a number of technological advances that have made life more convenient, including "dental and medical equipment, antibiotics, bypass operations, safe births, control of genetically transmitted diseases, personal computers, compact discs, television sets, automobiles, opportunities for fast and cheap world-wide travel, air conditioning..." And so on. For the record, I'm quite happy for all of these advances, yet I still don't see how anything on this list is addressing our self-inflicted mass extinction, though I suppose it's making us comfortable in the meantime.

I also see the invention of new technology as a response to a specific technical problem (or set of problems) rather than merely the offspring of pro-growth economic conditions.

What I find far more curious, though, is why Dr. Lipsey's sweeping claim avoids any mention of mass extinction or climate change. And, how did his opinion come to reflect the voice of so many high-profile public figures? It seems true enough that, as Lipsey writes, "...our Victorian ancestors could not have imagined what to do with ten times as much of all of the goods that they knew about." Yet it is also true that we have far more than ten times the goods those ancestors knew about, and our aggregate material footprint is still going up. Efficiency gains are a feel-good story, but the gains have yet to reduce our aggregate material footprint at the global level.

I'm not an ideological enemy of innovation or entrepreneurship. In fact, I'm a bit of a techno-geek—I (somewhat shamefully) enjoy new technologies and toys. I get irrationally excited when I see developments in green technology and transportation, and I've started a business. I can't wait to use a hyperloop. But, as Lewis and Conaty write in *The Resilience Imperative*, I embrace the principle that efficiency without sufficiency is lost. Or to put it another way, it feels intellectually dishonest to suggest that efficiency has the potential to deliver us from a cultural propensity for overconsumption. I'm not certain why we should focus our energy on miniaturizing goods or "cleaning" our production process to the exclusion of simply consuming less. We need both.

Underpinning some of Dr. Lipsey's claims is the assumption that innovation is merely a technological, material, or financial phenomenon. What precludes us from innovating ethically and socially toward more desirable ends? John Maynard Keynes considered the day when society could focus on happiness and well-being rather than economic growth. He wrote, "The day is not far off when the economic problem will take the back seat where it belongs, and the arena of the heart and the head will be occupied or reoccupied, by our real problems—the problems of life and of human relations, of creation and behavior and religion."

I also can't help but wonder if Dr. Lipsey recognizes that his narrative emerged during a time when one could not so readily see or feel the effects of a deteriorating planetary life support system. I don't blame him for his initial choice of narrative—like many 20th century thinkers, his whole identity was constructed to promote the idea of growth. But at some point, we will all need to accept our planetary prognosis and act accordingly.

It's become exceedingly clear that price signals alone won't preserve forests, oceans, or climate stability. By the time we've settled on a carbon price, the planet will already have become several degrees warmer, and we'll no longer have the luxury of technocratic tinkering. Behavioral economists have also debunked the myth that humans are motivated only by price signals. Human beings are complex, irrational actors who are influenced by far more than just the almighty dollar. Many of us have given up on the neoclassical paradigm precisely because of this new knowledge. Call it innovation.

It's not necessarily true anymore that economic growth increases our incomes and always transforms our lives for the better. Today, some features of economic growth are increasing the incomes of the richest, stagnating the incomes of the poorest, and depleting the innovative spirit of the economy. Who has the time to worry about climate change and mass extinction when they're just getting by or more concerned about how to cash their next pension check?

Perhaps we can be thankful that growth didn't stop in 1900 or 1950, as Dr. Lipsey argues. But this isn't 1950. We have to solve a new set of problems. There's never been a better time for innovation in the field of economics, even with our definition of progress.

References

Lewis, M, and P. Conaty. 2012. *The Resilience Imperative: Cooperative Transitions to a Steady-State Economy*. New Society Publishers, Grabiola Island, Canada.

A Steady-State Defense
of Arts and Culture

Politicians, pundits, and average people have increasingly antagonized artists to make what they do "accessible" and to legitimate their trade in monetary terms. In one infamous interview on an upstart Canadian news channel [the now defunct Sun News Network], hapless anchor Krista Erickson attacked one of the country's most prestigious contemporary dancers in a stunning display of vitriolic ignorance and objectionable theatrical bullying.

The pervasive (and especially North American) notion that the arts need to be assigned a monetary value in order to be legitimized is quite simply misplaced. Arts and culture provide intangible value to society; they transcend monetary values just as they transcend history. In a future clouded with economic and environmental uncertainty, materially lighter endeavors such as the arts should feature more prominently in society as we move towards a steady state.

Part of the problem is that the lines are often blurred between industrial mass culture and more traditional forms of culture. Populist commercial products that people can easily "access" will almost universally be more profitable. But what is popular and profitable is not necessarily artistic.

The so-called "elitist" art forms are the more endangered cultural species and in need of greater support and understanding. I'm talking about the ones that have intrinsic value as reflections of identity or history, like performances of cultural dance, taiko drumming, Chopin, jazz, or Inuit throat singing. These practices are not accessible to all people and will even be detestable to some, so their preservation requires that audiences put effort into understanding them. That's why so many trained artists have no choice but to share their craft as educators.

What about modern art? I can't defend contemporary stuff wholesale. Some will sink and some will swim. But whether it's a play written about a small community or a graphic that reflects nothing more than a mood, such artworks are created to show us something about ourselves—something to nurture our souls. That point is lost when you persistently have to defend their economic worth because, frankly, few of these things will ever be profitable in narrow monetary terms, and why should they be? Unlike mass culture, these creations are not intended to be accessible to the largest possible swath of humanity! But tax dollars are certainly not being "wasted" to support artists who are often almost obsessively dedicated to what they do, and seldom apply for grants in the first place.

So, beyond monetary terms, how can we come to understand the economic role of arts and culture? We should come to view the arts primarily as a subsistence endeavor which produces enough for artists to live simply and frugally. It's a form of voluntary simplicity much like subsistence farming or running a small business; precious little to criticize in a steady state economy. These endeavors don't demand much: they don't add to the debt burden, and they don't consume massive quantities of material or financial resources as they go about enriching our lives. Artists also often live in affordable geographic areas that are dilapidated (such as inner cities) and in need of the kind of vibrant renewal the arts provide. Artists in fact contribute far more to society than they consume.

Last but not least, what about the artistic product itself? If the product is not necessarily profit-producing, what legitimizes its worth? Some would argue that only endurance can legitimize the artistic product. As an impulsively self-gratifying, increasingly narcissistic society, the idea that we can only come to know something in time is a hard reality to accept. But some of these curious, inaccessible modern works will indeed become classics in time. Think of the 20th century works of Beckett or Joyce. They still aren't really accessible in that you have to work at understanding them, but they are remarkable creations and have to be respected for the way they hold a mirror to society.

It is the responsibility of both the artist and the average person to understand the socioeconomic contributions of the arts. Understanding and enjoying the arts is a lifestyle choice that will sometimes require us to get off the couch, step away from the television and into art galleries, music and dance halls, places of worship, and libraries. The process has the positive side effect of building stronger relationships and communities. Not everything we experience will be perfect (and some of it may be bad), but that's part of the adventure, because every now and then we will come across something that changes our perspective a little, or maybe a lot.

And there's never been a better time to start seeing things a little differently, especially when comparing monetary to non-monetary values!

Transition Winnipeg Embraces
the Steady State Economy

W hen activists, teachers, and thought leaders talk about the steady state economy, they often refer to macroeconomic, state-oriented policy. Not always fodder for dinner conversation. If we're going to mainstream steady-state economics, efforts have to be reflected in the local community to show what a steady state economy feels like in the real world. To that end, I believe a strategic partnership between the transition movement and steady-state advocates would be mutually beneficial.

Transition initiatives are in need of a lexicon that articulates what we're transitioning *to*; that is, the post-growth transition to a steady state economy. Then the steady-state movement would be able to foster greater collaboration with proponents of community economic development and grassroots change. In collaboration with a number of local teachers and practitioners, I tested a strategic partnership over the last two years with positive early results in a city that isn't generally known for post-growth thought.

Sometimes, steady staters simply fall into the trap of preaching to the wrong audience. We want to celebrate the adoption of steady-state policies by governments—things like the reduction of the work week, a basic income, and an increase in the fractional reserve requirement. Yet rather than having conversations with our neighbors, we jet-set to cosmopolitan centers only to argue with neoclassical macroeconomists over the feasibility of embracing a new set of norms. Among audiences where competitive overconsumption and entitlement are accepted as prime motivators, the steady state economy is no easy sell! The culture shift has to start elsewhere.

In fact, the culture shift is likely occurring among a sizeable number of citizens in your own community where steady-state policies are an easy sell indeed. Perhaps post-growth thinkers need to embrace a "both/and" strategy—both policy reform and grassroots change—rather than privileging one over the other or wasting energy on the wrong audience.

Enter the transition movement, a neighborhood-based movement for low-carbon, climate-resilient action and reform.

The transition movement has adopted the notion that, "If we try and do it on our own it will be too little, but if we wait for government to do it, it will be too late. So then, if we can gather together those around us—our street, our neighborhood, our community—it might just be enough, and it might just be in time." This likely resonates with proponents of degrowth towards a steady state economy, too. Clearly, if we wait for government it will be too late. If we act as individuals by embracing materially simpler lifestyles, we may just be branded "weird" by friends and family. That's too little. But if we foster a community of like-minded partners, our efforts may be just enough, just in time. Community gardens appear, a can-do entrepreneurial culture leaps ahead of fickle legislators, bottom-up pressure is exerted on bureaucrats, and simpler low-carbon lifestyles become almost cool—perhaps even hip(ster). More than anything else, the transition becomes something that people can feel. It's achievable, and it's fun!

Can it happen in your community? I think Transition Winnipeg's early experience demonstrates that it can happen just about anywhere. Over the past two years, I inflicted my enthusiasm for post-growth economic change upon the organization's initiating committee. What I found was that grassroots activists and practitioners were craving a word that described an economy that functions within ecological limits. Often the only word we use to describe the present state of affairs is "capitalism," but popular alternatives such as "socialism" aren't universally designed to function within ecological limits either. Enter the phrase "steady state economy," which resonates almost immediately. It may not imply a complete model of political economy, but it certainly covers the goal of functioning within ecological limits.

Transition Winnipeg's first pass at imagining Winnipeg as a thriving post-growth community and steady state economy is entitled *Winnipeg's Great Transition: Ideas and Actions for a Climate-Resilient, Low-Carbon City*. The document is not all that unique among transition initiatives. In fact, there are plenty of vision documents among transition towns, often called "energy descent action plans," that outline how energy and climate constraints will shape communities in the years to come. What is perhaps unique about *Winnipeg's Great Transition* is its explicit use of the post-growth paradigm and steady state economy as organizing principles. After all, energy use and economic growth have historically been extremely closely linked; it is accepted among ecological economists that you can't have much of one without the other. On many transition websites, including that of the REconomy Project, "growth" was widely used at first. While the term seems to have been phased out, "steady state" has not yet been embraced as an alternative. Would it not be meaningful for transition groups to state explicitly the goal of a steady state economy (or degrowth toward a steady state economy)?

The release of *Winnipeg's Great Transition* was something of a one-day sensation in the local media for a city where ecological resilience and post-growth planning almost never makes the headlines. We timed the release to coincide with the middle of the civic election and invited a number of mayoral candidates to attend. Three candidates joined us for a sincere dialogue and were receptive to the strategy. The authors of the report were invited by some of the candidates to provide a workshop to the new city council to explain why post-growth planning is important, and how it improves resilience. The report may even have made conversation around the dinner table.

Are small, local initiatives like ours going to move us toward a steady state economy overnight? No. Are they going to create the kind of on-the-ground connections and enthusiasm that a full-scale political and economic movement requires? With time, I believe they will.

Part VI

Eric Zencey

Two Schools and the Path
to the Steady State Economy

All of economics can be divided into two schools: steady-state theory and infinite-planet theory. They can't both be right. You'd think the choice between them would be obvious, but infinite-planet theory still holds sway in classrooms and in the halls of power where policies are made. Last month, though, brought a significant development: the manager of a major hedge fund registered a carefully reasoned dissent from infinite-planet theory. And in doing so, Jeremy Grantham offered a glimpse of how and why steady-state theory will ultimately come to prevail.

Grantham is the head of GMO LLC, a hedge fund with $100 billion under management. His latest letter to his investors was headlined "Time to Wake Up: Days of Abundant Resources and Falling Prices Are Over Forever." The title calls to mind the urgent warnings raised by steady staters as far back as the 1970s. The warnings were dismissed by most economists as Chicken-Little fears that could safely be ignored, and the western industrial world proceeded to do just that. Infinite-planet theorists pointed to the work of Julian Simon, who argued that human ingenuity is "the ultimate resource." Because human capacity for invention was infinite, there could be no resource limits to economic growth.

You can get to that conclusion only if you ignore basic physics. However inventive humans have been or may yet prove to be, they'll never invent a way around the first and second laws of thermodynamics. You can't make something from nothing, and you can't make nothing from something (first law). You can't push a car backwards to refill the gas tank (second law). Together these laws rule out perpetual motion schemes whereby energy is "created" or recycled and used again.

In steady-state theory, the economy is seen as a thermodynamic machine, processing matter and energy and leaving a high-entropy wake. The economy thus has two ecological footprints: one on the uptake and one from the discharge. Since both footprints land outside the abstract world of theory and in the physical reality of a finite planet, neither can increase forever.

Economists might have put these truths into practice decades ago. Had they done so, they would have been in good company. Physics had its thermodynamic revolution in the person of Albert Einstein, whose path from Newton to relativity began with thermodynamics, as he sorted out the non-mechanical aspects of the second law. (Mechanical motion is reversible; energy use is not.)

Meanwhile biology was transformed in the 1920s and 1930s as biologists saw that evolution is driven by competition for energy, which structures and maintains food webs, in which the process of photosynthesis begets green plant then herbivore, carnivore, and eventually detritivore.

Why, then, has the thermodynamic revolution in economics been postponed? The question will intrigue historians of the future, who will wonder at the profligacy of our culture and our cavalier disregard for ecological limits.

Part of the answer is the bet that Julian Simon made in 1980 with population activist Paul Ehrlich. Simon maneuvered Ehrlich into wagering on the future price of any group of resources that Ehrlich cared to pick: if Simon's theory was right, he claimed, the prices would be lower within ten years. Simon won.

His victory was widely taken as proof of his infinite-planet theory, despite the obvious flaw in it. The market price of any commodity is a human construct, the result of market supply and demand, not an indicator of scarcity in any absolute sense. From a limited stock of a finite resource—oil, say—we can choose to extract the resource at a greater or lesser rate. If the rate at which we pump oil out of the ground exceeds the rate at which demand for oil increases, the market price will fall. This doesn't prove that oil is plentiful, let alone infinite. It doesn't prove that we've invented our way around the laws of thermodynamics. It merely proves that we've extracted oil fast enough to keep its market price from rising.

Now Grantham goes head-to-head with Simon's vision, and on (the late) Simon's own terms. Commodity prices are rising. Of course, many commodity prices are notoriously volatile. Sharp increases in the prices of significant commodities since 2002 fall well outside the standard deviation; for iron ore, the rise has been 4.9 times the standard deviation, a result that (Grantham tells us) has a one in 2.2 million chance of being "normal" variation. More likely, it signals a new and different reality. For coal, copper, corn, silver, sorghum, palladium, rubber, etc., the odds aren't as long, but still quite sizable, ranging from one to 48,000 (coal) to one in 4,000 (rubber). This basic, deep-seated trend lies beneath the statistical noise—price spikes and troughs, including those created by speculation and subsequent "market corrections."

Based on this analysis, and on a review of energy use that reaches back to when wood was our primary fuel, Grantham concludes that we have entered a new era: we are on the cusp of what he calls The Great Paradigm Shift, claiming it is "one of the giant inflection points in economic history." The moment, he warns, that lies at "the beginning of the end for the heroic growth spurt in population and wealth caused by...the Hydrocarbon Revolution."

You don't find too many economists, let alone market analysts, reaching back to look at energy use before the era of coal. In the infinite-planet neoclassical model, anything before James Watt is quaint and distant, and everything before Adam Smith is simply darkness. It's true enough that steam-driven factories, embodying the division of labor that Smith celebrated, were game changers, leading to phenomenal economic growth. However, you can't appreciate the "game," or even begin to see that it has an end, unless you put those inventions into a historical and geophysical perspective that reaches back before Watt and Smith.

That's why the Industrial Revolution is more properly called the Hydrocarbon Revolution. In focusing on the machinery, "Industrial Revolution" leads us to think that the engine of economic growth was human invention—and thus leads to the mistaken idea that more and better invention will let us increase productivity forever. "Hydrocarbon Revolution" makes clear that the modern economic "miracle" has natural, thermodynamic roots. Economic history changed when we began systematically to exploit a new stock of energy, the stored fossil sunlight of coal and oil, with its historically unprecedented rate of energy return on energy invested (EROI)—as high as 100:1 for oil in the early part of the twentieth century. "Hydrocarbon Revolution" reflects the reality that the enormous productivity gains of the machine age are rooted in that very favorable EROI. It also implicitly includes the warning that the modern economic miracle must end when this stock of thermodynamically cheap energy is used up.

The essence of steady-state thinking is that we have to shape our economy to operate on a finite planet, within a stable, sustainable budget of matter-and-energy throughput. That throughput has to be sized so that the economy's two footprints fit into the available ecological shoes. Grantham has noticed that one of the shoes is pinching, and he's begun to articulate the reasons why, to an audience highly motivated to listen. If they heed his warning that, "From now on, price pressure and shortages of resources will be a permanent feature of our lives," the psychological engine of self-interest will be hitched to the adoption of steady-state economic theory.

Upton Sinclair once observed, "It is difficult to get a man to understand something when his salary depends upon his not understanding it." In the past that logic has worked against the spread of steady-state thinking, but the logic is entering a new historic context, which hasn't escaped Grantham. If you want to make money, he avers, you'd better acknowledge reality, including the reality that on a finite planet there are limits to growth. This is a welcome development, even to those of us less concerned with money-making than with the fate of a civilization that's outgrown its ecological niche.

China's Infinite-Growth Haze

A few weeks ago, air quality at the U.S. embassy in Beijing registered roughly 750 on a scale accurately calibrated to only 500. A thick, choking haze enveloped the entire city. You couldn't see from one high-rise office tower to the next; flights were cancelled, some highways were closed, schoolchildren were kept indoors, and hospital admissions soared. China's air quality problems aren't limited to Beijing. A 2010 study found that air pollution led to 1.2 million premature deaths nationwide, and killer air is just one of the country's ecological sorrows. Half of its surface water is so polluted it can't be treated to make it drinkable, and half of that is so bad it can't even be used for industrial purposes. Seventy percent of the country's rivers and lakes receive raw sewage or untreated industrial toxins. Cancer rates are up, and the country has been losing an area the size of Connecticut every year to desertification, brought on by unsustainable farming practices in grassland ecosystems.

In protest, Chinese people have begun taking to the streets in demonstrations that have increasingly become clashes, sometimes bloody, with riot police.

Between 1978 and 2008 the Chinese economy grew tenfold, outpacing the rest of the world. (In comparison, U.S. real GDP tripled in that period.) The growth has come at considerable and notorious cost in contaminated air and water and other "disamenities" such as pulmonary disease, cancer, and riots.

Are these the necessary costs of development? Of course not. So why is China paying them? As with most real-world questions there is no single answer, but one of the clearest, strongest, and saddest parts of a complete answer is this: China listened to the wrong economists.

Those economists are neither crazy nor blind. They can see the human cost of pollution and environmental degradation. But they've got a theory that reassures them the problem is only temporary and will fix itself: the Environmental Kuznets Curve (EKC). Pursuant to the EKC, pollution levels are (of course) low before "development" occurs. Pollution increases as economic activity and income rise. However, at some tipping point (the highest point on the curve), pollution peaks and thenceforth declines with additional income, because a wealthier population demands and can afford more environmental quality.

This, the standard economics textbooks say, is "intuitively appealing." And it is—if your intuition has been shaped by traditional economic theory. If ecological damage can always be reversed, and if environmental quality isn't a God-given gift or a basic human right but a commodity like any other, then it makes sense to think that you can buy a better environment when you get more income. The implication is that "Growth is the Key to Protecting the Environment, Not its Enemy," as one article on the EKC puts it.

EKC logic leads to an absurd conclusion (always a bad sign for a theory): The reason we have climate change is that the richest countries the planet has ever seen are still not rich enough to afford the environmental good known as "climate stability." Nor can the EKC be defended on empirical grounds as good science. The *New Palgrave Dictionary of Economics* acknowledges that most EKC studies "are designed to yield inverse-U-shaped pollution-income paths and succeed using a variety of assumptions and mechanisms." In other words, most EKC studies are more consistent with the preservation of pro-growth faith than with scientific inquiry.

While the inverted U of the EKC does describe the relationship between some key pollutants and GDP growth in some developed countries, that finding has fatal conceptual flaws. "Key" pollutants are not all pollutants, and particular pollutants aren't the sole and permanent marker of ecological degradation. Policies that control one kind of pollutant (and which thereby send its EKC down) may simply encourage a shift to manufacturing processes that produce other kinds of pollutants—ones that aren't (yet) regulated and haven't ever been measured, so there's no possible way to chart their history on an EKC.

Another kind of shift establishes an EKC for a pollutant in one country because the manufacturing process itself moves to another country. If exporting a dirty industrial process to a "pollution haven" with little or no regulation is cheaper than meeting regulatory standards at home, why would a profit-maximizing company do anything else? And, if a nation's primary policy goal is GDP growth, why would it deter such a profit-maximizing operation by regulating the pollution?

In the political effort to shift a wealthy country's pollution to another country, the EKC is a big help. It reassures the recipient country that poisoned air and water are a necessary phase of economic development, and that someday the recipient country, too, will be rich enough to restore the environmental quality it once had. What the EKC doesn't address is that ecosystems can be degraded past any possibility of repair or reclamation. It doesn't remind anyone that extinct species are gone for good. It takes no heed of the fact that we live on a finite planet, and eventually there are no more pollution-haven countries left for exporting the dirty industries to.

In 2005 Pan Yue, then China's vice minister of environmental protection, lamented his country's acceptance of the EKC: "The assumption [was] that the economic growth [we pursued] will give us the financial resources to cope with the crises surrounding the environment, raw materials, and population growth" (Lorenz 2005). And China's pollution is only one shoe of its ecological footprint. The other shoe comes down in lockstep, as China scours the globe for farmland and other natural resources (most notably in Africa and South America).

Yet, to this day, the EKC is standard fare in neoclassical economics. Isn't it time to stop seeing the world through the distorting, poisonous haze of an unsupportable theory, and to start seeing the world as it actually is? China is no mere clue!

References

Lorenz, A. 2005. SPIEGEL Interview with China's deputy minister of the environment: "The Chinese miracle will end soon." *SPIEGEL Online* 10, March 7, 2005.

Slumlord Nation

According to architectural critic Charles Jencks, modern architecture died on March 16, 1972. That's the day that dynamite charges brought down the first of the Pruitt-Igoe public housing towers in St. Louis, Missouri. You've probably seen the pictures: a cloud of dust swirls out into the street while the tops of the buildings, still square, sag and tilt crazily. The photo captures rectilinear form giving way to nebulous dust and rubble. This iconic image reminds us that entropy—the law of increasing disorder—haunts all our acts and works. In the distance you can make out another St. Louis icon, Eero Saarinen's Gateway Arch, that gleaming stainless steel monument to the city's role as mustering yard for the nation's western expansion.

Jencks was wrong about modern architecture. So are those who blamed the residents of Pruitt-Igoe for the buildings' decay and destruction. What brought those buildings down is a dynamic that's ever present in our modern economies—a dynamic that the conceptual lens of ecological economics lets us see very clearly.

Pruitt-Igoe was a federally funded urban renewal project comprising of thirty-three high-rise apartment buildings, eleven stories each, on a fifty-seven acre plot. It represented the best design practices for high-density urban development when it was built. It had green space (a benefit of building up instead of out). It had community function rooms on the ground floor and every third floor, which is where the novel, skip-stop elevators went, encouraging residents to think of every three floors as a neighborhood (as they'd encounter and meet each other in the intervening stairwells).

Within the limits of Missouri law, it was desegregated. The Pruitt towers, named for a black WWII aviator from Missouri, were for blacks, and the Igoe towers, named for a white Congressman, were for whites. The whole complex was designed for mixed incomes. Some apartments were rented at market rates to middle class families; others were subsidized, with rent limited to a percentage of household income. (Under welfare rules, these apartments could not have telephones or televisions and were available only to families that did not have an able-bodied wage-earner in the household.)

New and ultra-modern when they were built in the early 1950s, after less than two decades' use the buildings had become a filthy, crime-infested, broken-windowed, high-rise slum, as bad as (and in many ways worse than) the housing they had been built to replace. In desperation the St. Louis Housing Authority consolidated the remaining tenants into a few buildings and demolished the others. The attempt at retrenchment failed. By 1976 the last remaining tenants had been relocated, the buildings razed, the site bulldozed. Today the acreage holds a couple of schools and the country's largest accidental urban forest.

What brought the towers down, says one conventional narrative, was the behavior of its residents. Despite the plan for a mix of income groups and separate-but-close mingling of races, the towers soon held just low-income African Americans, and they were responsible for trashing the buildings. The architect, Minoru Yamasaki (who later designed the World Trade Center Towers) gave credence to this racially charged interpretation when he allowed, "I never thought people were that destructive" (Marshall 2015). A less racist version of this narrative adds that adolescent boys are always the prime perpetrators of vandalism, and that welfare regulations had the unintended effect of breaking up families, ensuring that quite a few adolescent males in the complex had no father figure at home. Vandalism and crime were the predictable result.

A different conventional narrative is told by some architectural critics, like Jencks, who find that the building themselves were at fault. The projects were too massive, too anonymous, too soulless to be successful in fostering neighborliness and a shared sense of pride in place. The public spaces of the complex, this theory says, became no-man's lands that residents avoided and hurried through. With no one caring for them, they fell into disrepair and bred crime, vandalism, trash, and brutality.

Neither of those narratives comes anywhere close to capturing the complex truth, which is that the Pruitt-Igoe towers were brought down by an unfortunate collision of factors. Federal funding paid for construction, but operating costs were the responsibility of the city. The intended occupancy rate would have enabled rental income to cover these. But the population of

St. Louis was undergoing an historic change; it fell from 857,000 to 622,000 between 1950 and 1970. Some of this was a general postwar exodus to the suburbs, fueled by cheap gas, Veterans Administration mortgages, and the assembly-line methods of suburban construction pioneered in Levittown. Some—a great part of it—was white flight. In 1954 the Supreme Court's decision in *Brown v. Board of Education of Topeka* mandated the desegregation of public schools, and two years later a Missouri court ordered desegregation of public housing in the city. Middle-class whites left St. Louis for the suburbs, where housing costs and racial discrimination in sales and rentals—"redlining"—would preserve segregated schools for decades to come. With its middle-income apartments emptying and being re-let to impoverished black families, the Housing Authority could no longer support Pruitt-Igoe's maintenance expenses.

The slum housing that Pruitt-Igoe replaced had become degraded and unhealthy for sound economic reasons. A slumlord maximizes his income stream by zeroing out maintenance costs, consuming the stored integrity of a building as income, and letting the building depreciate down to nothing. Tax law, which allows deductions for depreciation, makes this an even more lucrative strategy. Faced with an inadequate income stream, the public housing authority of St. Louis did what slumlords do: they reduced their budget gap by zeroing out maintenance expenses and sucking the integrity and usefulness out of their property.

As any businessman can tell you, if your operation can't afford routine maintenance of its productive assets, your operation is in deep trouble. What you've got then isn't a business plan, but a parasitic plan; a plan to be a parasite.

Nature knows three kinds of parasites. One lives in a symbiotic relationship with its host, never diverting so much of the host's life-energy as to constitute a threat to its continued well-being. (You don't even notice the mites that live on your dead skin cells.) Another kind of parasite flourishes by consuming its host to death; like smallpox or the plague, it destroys what it feeds on and then jumps to another host. A third kind of parasite falls in between. It sucks a considerable amount of life from the host but doesn't actually kill it; it achieves a kind of equilibrium, imposing a degraded and diminished life on its host. Tapeworms fall into this category, along with some chronic diseases, such as leprosy, malaria, and tuberculosis. Call it the slumlord model: sustainable, under certain conditions.

Unlike the things humans build, ecosystems (and, by and large, individual organisms within them) are capable of a high degree of self-repair. Any act of maintenance involves resisting entropic decline in a system by importing matter, energy, and design intelligence into a system to restore a valued

116

and orderly arrangement. Broken windows don't fix themselves. For that you need new glass and a glazier to install it. But damaged ecosystems do repair themselves, if they haven't been degraded beyond recovery. They use physical nutrients, solar throughput, and the design intelligence of evolution to maintain and deepen their systems of orderly relations.

In his 1952 classic *Soil and Civilization*, Edward Hyams pointed out that humans have always been parasites on their host ecosystems. We divert some of the resource-energy of those systems and channel it through our bodies and societies before exhausting it, degraded, back into the host. Many, even most hunter-gatherer tribes lived in symbiotic relationship with ecosystems, colonizing part of nature's food-energy flow but rarely threatening the integrity and continued life of the system as a whole. As agriculturalists, humans sometimes lived in balance with the soil community, not extracting more of its fertility than the system could rebuild from annual solar inflow. But some agricultural societies mined their soil fertility, drawing it down faster than it could be replenished. They consumed the maintenance-energy of their host soils, and either jumped to another host or disappeared as their once-fertile land became sterile sand and gravel.

Today, much of humanity functions as hydrocarbon-fueled industrial parasites—life-suckers whose ambitions include not just food security and reproduction but the accumulation of great material wealth. To gratify those ambitions, we've used the stored capital of the planet (a finite stock of fossil fuels) to increase the rate at which we suck the maintenance out of planetary ecosystems. We've become a slumlord species: we cash out nature's maintenance flows and spend our gains as income.

Symbiotic parasitism, which allows the host to flourish, is the only one of these roles that will give us an ecologically sustainable economy with a relatively high standard of living. The find-another-host strategy is clearly out: we've only got one planet, and we've built out to the edge of its capacity to hold us. The slumlord strategy won't work, either. The typical slumlord doesn't have to live in the slum that his self-interested behavior creates; his home is somewhere else. On a fully developed, fully occupied planet, there is no "somewhere else."

Once upon a time, when the world held fewer humans, it seemed there was room for slumlord parasitism. Saarinen's Gateway Arch memorializes an epic transit, the opening of the American West, and it's fitting that you can see it on the distant horizon in those iconic pictures of the Pruitt-Igoe demolition. Whatever else it memorializes, the Arch also marks the transit of a parasitic species looking for a new host, migrating in search of fresh ecosystems whose stocks of capital and maintenance energy could be sucked down, cashed out and spent as current income.

Eventually some humans learned that we ought not to turn our own environmental neighborhood into a slum. Many developed nations passed laws; in the U.S. there was the Clean Air Act, Clean Water Act, Endangered Species Act and others to ensure that we didn't cancel out the maintenance of the ecosystems that support us. But like slumlords comfortably housed in the suburbs, those in the industrialized countries continued to benefit from the draw-down of maintenance elsewhere on the planet. We in the USA, especially, exported our damage to the undeveloped and less developed nations of the world, nations that sacrificed natural capital and ecosystem integrity to the promise—often unfulfilled—of economic gain.

In St. Louis, slumlords depended on the existence of a class of renters who had no other choices. Poverty and racism held African Americans in place, in housing that no one should have to endure. In the world at large, our slumlord practice is maintained by the dogma of infinite-planet economics. We rely on the ideology of free trade, and the spurious argument that environmental quality is a luxury good, to tell the impoverished citizens of the world that if they're patient enough and smart enough, they will someday live as we do—as if a political economy in which 5 percent of the world's population uses 25 percent of the world's resource flow could be expanded to include everyone.

For now there is just enough material progress to support the dogma. Thanks to the frantic expansion of the matter and energy streams that humans suck from the planet, and to a decline in the U.S. share of that stream as its middle class disappears, once-poor countries like China and India are developing their own middle-class consumerist economies. Meanwhile, our planetary habitat is damaged and degraded even more rapidly. To most of our untrained eyes, most areas look reasonably okay, but that's only because we haven't been schooled in the ecological understanding required to assess the damage. Our ecological ignorance "helps" us to ignore the fact that we're sucking the life-maintenance out of the planet.

The fate of the Pruitt-Igoe towers—memorialized in that iconic photo from 1972—shows us the likely outcome of such "help."

References

Marshall, C. 2015. Pruitt-Igoe: the troubled high-rise that came to define urban America—a history of cities in 50 buildings, day 21. *The Guardian*, April 22, 2015.